José Ignacio Rodríguez

**The Case of the Arrest, Trial and Sentence in the City of**

**Havana**

José Ignacio Rodríguez

**The Case of the Arrest, Trial and Sentence in the City of Havana**

ISBN/EAN: 9783337379230

Printed in Europe, USA, Canada, Australia, Japan

Cover: Foto ©ninafisch / pixelio.de

More available books at **www.hansebooks.com**

# THE CASE

OF ·THE

## ARREST, TRIAL AND SENTENCE IN THE CITY OF HAVANA, ISLAND OF CUBA

OF

## JULIO SANGUILY

A CITIZEN OF THE UNITED STATES OF AMERICA

BY

## JOSÉ IGNACIO RODRIGUEZ

COUNSEL FOR THE PRISONER IN THE
CITY OF WASHINGTON

WASHINGTON, D. C.
PRESS OF W. F. ROBERTS
1897

# THE CASE

## OF THE ARREST, TRIAL AND SENTENCE IN THE CITY OF HAVANA, ISLAND OF CUBA, OF

# JULIO SANGUILY,

## A CITIZEN OF THE UNITED STATES OF AMERICA.

The case of JULIO SANGUILY, a citizen of the United States of America, arrested and tried in Havana, Island of Cuba, on a charge of political character, did not begin to attract, to any practical extent at least, the attention of the people in this country, until after it had gone successfully through its most dangerous stages.

Fortunately for the prisoner, the action in his favor of Mr. Richard Olney, Secretary of State of the United States of America, at all times prompt, patriotic and energetic, and the action of his lawyers in Washington, and in Havana, as well as in Madrid, always firm, calm, conscientious, inspired by no other sentiment than the good of their client and absolutely and completely disinterested, were never hampered, to any amount worth mentioning, by outside interposition of any kind, until the very moment in which, through skillful diplomatic management, the release of Sanguily from imprisonment, without further suffering or humiliation, had been secured.

But that moment was one of extreme perplexity, which the friends of Sanguily will not easily forget. Through an exuberant effusion of patriotic zeal and most commendable humanitarian feelings on the part of certain members of the United States Senate;—through a noble, although misguided, sentiment of generous compassion, industriously worked up in their minds, and in the minds of the kind hearted people of this country, by wilful misrepresentation of the facts of the case, and by stories propagated by false friends and intruders about wrongs and sufferings and indignities perpetrated upon the prisoner, which in fact were never perpetrated or attempted to be perpetrated ;—through the desire of certain Cuban agitators, without authority to speak for the prisoner, of posing as his friends, urging extreme measures, and precipitating, if possible, a conflict between the United States and Spain, aiming at no other end and seeking no other thing than the advance of the cause in the advocation of which they were engaged ;—through the temptation into which many a distinguished public man of this country seemed to have been led of converting a case, which involved the liberty and perhaps the life of a citizen of the United States of America, into an instrument of opposition to the ideas and principles represented by President Cleveland and his Secretary of State, Mr. Olney ;—through the vocifera-tion of certain part of the press ;—and through many other causes and circumstances, a condition of things, which might have proved fatal, was created at once.  A measure of doubtful justice, and of more than questionable efficiency, calculated perhaps more to irritate Spain and embroil the United States of America in a war with that nation, than to save Sanguily, and grounded upon an imperfect knowledge of the facts of the case, was attempted to be rushed through the United States Senate, exactly at the same time in which the determination already reached by Spain to comply with the wishes of the United States of America and set Julio Sanguily at liberty was being carried into execution.

Thanks to Divine Providence, through the righteous attitude of the State Department ;—through the firm stand of some Honorable Senators, who were then called " organs of the Governor-General of Cuba, or of the Queen of Spain," and against whom the friends of the measure acknowledged to have used " a little

by-word of bandinage ;" through the cooperation of the Spanish
Minister ; and perhaps through the earnest appeal of the prisoner's counsel to the Honorable Chairman of the Senate Committee on Foreign Relations,—the crisis was averted, and the
most gracious act of Her Majesty the Queen Regent of Spain,
to whom Sanguily personally was not absolutely a stranger, (*)
could be carried into effect in Havana, without the slightest
difficulty.

When the echo of the speeches which were made in the
Senate and of the applauses which their most fiery passages
had elicited from the galleries, had not as yet died out, Sanguily, already a free man, was joining his family, and prepar-
ing to leave the Island of Cuba.

Warm hearts and cool heads had once more overpowered the
furies of blind excitement.

As an Honorable Senator, who represents in part in the
Federal Congress one of the most enlightened and law abiding
States of this powerful Union,—a State, however, which has the
misfortune of being in this respect a house divided within itself,
as the other Honorable Senator who completes its representa-
tion in that high body radically differs from his colleague in
many matters of importance,—did not hesitate to declare in the

---

(*) Subsequently to the compromise which put an end to the Cuban war
of independence of 1868-1878, Sanguily went to Spain and had the honor
to be presented in Madrid to Her Majesty the Queen Regent. She was
pleased to have with him a long conference, in which she treated him
with the utmost kindness. She invited him to be seated during the
whole time he was in her presence, and asked him many questions about
himself, about his wounds, about Cuba, and about the motives which
had prompted him to go to war against Spain. Noticing that he inad-
vertently had omitted in one of his answers to address her as "Your
Majesty," and had used the ordinary Spanish "Usted," equivalent
to the English "you," a mistake which somewhat embarrassed him
for a moment, she told him with a smile not to give her any more her
Royal title of honor. And when dismissing him, and wishing him good
health and prosperity, she gave him the permission to write to her,
directly, whenever he desired to have some favor granted, and indicated
the channel through which his communication should reach her hands.

4

effervescence of his rhetoric that the action of Sanguily's lawyer had been "exceedingly wicked and unjust;" (*) as the discussion in the Senate during the stormy session of the 25th of February, 1897, evinced a most extraordinary misapprehension of facts, which it is important to correct; as the principles of law, both international and municipal, involved in the case have not been settled and in all probability shall have again to be discussed; as the interest which this case has excited justifies a professional inquiry into its merits, a study of its features in its judicial as well as in its diplomatic branch, and a comparison between it and other cases of analogous character which are historical and to which both the United States Government and the Government of Spain were parties ; and as the necessity to do justice to whom justice is due is recognized by all, specially amidst the fair minded righteous communities which form this Union,—the writer of the present pages has not deemed to be improper to appear before the public and submit them to its judgment.

May they be read in the same spirit of abhorrence of injustice in all its forms, and of love of truth, pure unsophisticated truth, in which they have been written.

I

THE ARREST OF SANGUILY, ITS CAUSES, REAL AND ALLEGED, AND THE CIRCUMSTANCES UNDER WHICH IT WAS MADE.

Julio Sanguily, a Cuban by birth, and a man of great prominence in the Cuban War of Independence of 1868–1878, in which he served with particular distinction as a Cuban Major General and had occasion to display very often his exceptional military ability and his almost legendary courage, was arrested in his house, in the city of Havana, Island of Cuba, where he had been living for some years in union with his family, at

(*) MR. WILLIAM P. FRYE, from Maine. Congressional Record, February 25, 1897. Page 2383.

about seven o'clock in the morning of Sunday the 24th of February, 1895.

This arrest, which had been ordered by the Governor-General of Cuba, on the ground which will be explained hereafter, was made quietly, without any unnecessary display of force or harsh treatment, but on the contrary with as much respectful consideration towards the prisoner as it was posible under the circumstances, by Colonel Don José Paglieri, the Chief of the Havana Police, upon whom it had befallen to fulfill such an unpleasant duty.

Sanguily was taken in a carriage from his home to the Police Headquarters, where he was seen by his brother, a distinguished Cuban scholar and jurist, and from there he was transferred, a short while afterwards to Fortress *La Cabaña*, where he was left, locked up in a cell or casemate, to await the action of a court martial.

To understand this arrest, as well as others which were made contemporarily, the fact must not be forgotten that the day before, Saturday the 23d of February, 1895, the whole territory of the Island of Cuba had been placed practically under the empire of Martial Law. Upon the ground that "a few ungrateful men, impelled by immeasurable ambition, having no worthy flag, and assisted and seconded perhaps by people unfriendly to labor, and even by criminals, were inviting a civil war, the greatest calamity which can befall a civilized people," His Excellency Don Emilio Calleja é Isasi, a Lieutenant-General in the Spanish Army and then the Governor-General of the Island, had issued on that date, a solemn proclamation, as usual in such cases, suspending practically all constitutional guarantees, and directing the so-called *Law of Public Order* of April 23d, 1870, to be put in operation and enforced at once as the paramount law of the land, throughout the whole Cuban territory.

A translation into English of the said proclamation and of some important articles of the *Law of Public Order* referred to by it, transmitted to the State Department by Mr. R. O. Williams the United States Consul-General at Havana, with his dispatch of February 26th, 1895, and printed in Document No. 224 of the House of Representatives, 54th Congress, 1st session, pages 13 to 15, shows to what extent, under the spur of self defense and public safety the powers of the Governor-General had then been stretched. Whether this measure was wise ; whether it was taken under a misapprehension of the magnitude of the movement or its intrinsic force; whether it was inspired by that feeling of distrust which lies at the very bottom of all the troubles between Spain and Cuba ; whether it served only, through inaugurating an era of violence which in its subsequent developments has tantalized the world, to infuse life into a movement which was not born in the country, which when imported there found no followers, which needed to be " rammed down through the throats of the people as the load of a musket is rammed into its barrel ", (*) and which, if successful as far as the annihilating almost totally the resources and the wealth of Cuba is concerned, has owed its success exclusively to Spanish mistakes, prompted by criminal pride or blindness (†),—are questions which do not belong to this

-----

(*) The words quoted in the text are a correct translation of those uttered in Spanish, in a moment of anger and disappointment, by the Dominican Máximo Gomez when after invading the province of Puerto Principe he saw no disposition on the part of the people to join him.

(†)Consul-General Williams in forwarding to the State Department the translations referred to in the text said: "The insurrectional movements that have given rise to the measures of the Governor-General seem to be limited to a very small number of persons, as shown by the prompt action of the three political parties engrossing the greatest part of the population and really representing the entire planting, industrial and commercial interests, as well as the professional classes of the Island; though it cannot be denied that poverty induced by the cumulative effects of the erroneous economic system long established here has brought about discontent among the working classes, since the principal exportable productions of the Island, sugar and tobacco are very depressed in their exchangeable values. This has brought on low and precarious wages,

place and are not attempted to be discussed here. But the fact
that it was taken, and that through it the situation of Cuba
was changed from one of orderly administration of law into
another of military rule and more or less ruthless violence,
must necessarily be borne in mind, if a complete idea of all the
circumstances attending this case is to be formed intelligently.

In justice to Governor General Calleja it must be stated also
that this method adopted by him to deal with the situation in
Cuba, and this arresting people and lodging them in fortresses
for alleged sympathies with rebels, without paying extra attention to individual rights, was not a novel process, exclusively
Spanish, or the invention of which was traceable to him
personally. In no country in the civilized world situations of
this character fail to present themselves together with the
circumstances out of which they arise. And even in these
United States, where individual liberty is not a theory but an
actual fact, where the individual citizen is the master and the
constituted authorities, even the highest in the social order,
acknowledge without difficulty that they are the servants, and
where the man who is naturally inclined to vex and tyrannize his
fellow being is rather an uncommon exception, the exhibition of
arbitrariness and rash proceedings, when the moment of danger

---

while at the same time important provisions and clothing are very high,
and in unfavorable disproportion to the earnings of the workmen."—
Doc. No. 224, House of Representatives, 54th Congress, 1st session, page
14.

Marshall Martinez Campos in one of his speeches in the Spanish Senate,
explained that *hunger* had been and continued to be a cause of the pro-
gress of the war in Cuba.—"More than 50,000 men," he said, "at Las
Villas and at Matanzas had been left (when the war commenced) without
a mouthful of bread and without resources of any kind, as the preceding
crop had scarcely yielded what was necessary to meet the expenses,
and as all work for the present one had been suspended. There being in
the country no saving habits, no cooperative associations, nothing which
could relieve the situation, the forced idleness of these men turned to be
a serious affliction, which imparts to the rebellion, specially at this moment, when all work in the small farms has been given up, a most
pavorous character."—(*El Pais*, Habana, July 28, 1896.)

arrived, might challenge comparison. If the Appleton American Annual Cyclopædia, volume corresponding to 1861, article Habeas Corpus, states the truth, the situation which existed in this country, as far as individual liberty was concerned, when the war of the secession broke out, might serve to demonstrate, if demonstration should be needed, that human nature is always the same, and that it ends after all by asserting itself. The article above cited contains a full description of the proceedings resorted to at that time, and a list of the citizens, 175 in number, who were arrested and transported to Fort Lafayette, N. Y., between the 20th of July and the 19th of October 1861, without authority of law, by mere executive decree, which in many cases consisted simply in a telegraphic order.

It must be stated also that the apprehensions felt by the Governor-General, as set forth in his proclamation, soon proved to be well founded ;—and that no longer period than twenty-four hours was required to elapse, before the dreadful calamity to which he had referred put in its appearance. The fact must not be forgotten that on that memorable 24th of February, 1895, on which Sanguily was arrested, the revolution which now counts fifty-two months of existence broke out in Cuba.

According to an affidavit, or certified statement, of Governor-General Calleja, dated March 25th, 1895, on file in the record of the case, the arrest of SANGUILY was ordered upon confidential reports, which convinced the Governor-General that the prisoner had been conspiring against the Government of Spain, and was to throw his sword and the prestige of his name in the cause of the rebellion.

These are the textual words of the affidavit: "As to Don Julio Sanguily and Don José María Aguirre, it is known to me, through confidential communications, both from this capital (Havana) and from abroad, that they were promoters of the separatist rebellion, and that it was said that they were to place themselves at the head of the insurrectionary movement

in the provinces of Havana, Matanzas and Santa Clara. That
their whole conduct which was closely watched by the police
also proved this. And that it was certain that they maintained relations and correspondence with the revolutionary
Junta at New York, with the workingmen abroad (meaning
probably the Cuban cigarmakers of Key West, Tampa, and
other cities of the United States of America) and with the
separatist committees of the provinces of the Island of Cuba.
Lastly, that by the same confidential channel I have received
more evidence concerning their operations, and particularly
their participation in the acquisition of munitions of war; but
as these proofs are given in confidential communications, I
abstain from making them public." (Doc. No. 104, Senate,
54th Congress, 2nd Session, page 56.)

This Don José María Aguirre, to whom the affidavit refers,
is the same José MARÍA TIMOTEO AGUIRRE, citizen of the
United States of America, who was arrested in Havana, on the
same day as Sanguily, just at the moment in which he was
boarding a train to go to the country, who through the
earnest efforts of the United States Government was released
from imprisonment on September 5th of the same year and sent
to New York, who immediately afterwards went back to Cuba
to command the insurgent forces of the province of Matanzas,
and who recently died there.

The correspondence in regard to the case of Mr. Aguirre,—
and also to the case of Mr. Francisco Carrillo, another Cuban
naturalized in the United States of America, arrested on February 27th, 1895, released through the interposition of the
State Department on May 30th of the same year, and now
fighting in Cuba,—can be found in Document No. 224, House
of Representatives, 54th Congress, 1st Session, from pages 90
to 111, and 133 to 144, respectively.

## II

### AMERICAN INTERPOSITION.

It is shown by the record that in the afternoon of the same day on which JULIO SANGUILY was arrested, his brother Don Manuel Sanguily, called at the residence of Mr. R. O. Williams, United States Consul General at Havana, brought to his attention that the prisoner was an American citizen by naturalization, and requested him to intervene in his favor.

Mr. Williams, who had not been that day at the Consulate, because it was Sunday, went at once to ascertain upon examination of his books whether the American citizenship, invocated by Sanguily's brother, was well established; and he found that in fact Julio Sanguily had been admitted to be a citizen of the United States of America by a decree of the Superior Court of the City of New York dated August 6th, 1878, that he had gone to Cuba with an American passport dated on the following day, that upon his arrival in Havana he had registered himself at the Consulate as an American, and that the Governor General of the Island had provided him with a certificate of identity, or *cédula personal* as it is called, dated August 22nd, 1878, wherein his American national character was recognized.

Upon this evidence, and in fulfillment of his duty, Mr. Williams prepared himself right away to bring these facts to the knowledge of Governor-General Calleja, and request him to extend to the prisoner all the rights and privileges secured by treaty for the citizens of the United States of America, when arrested and tried in Spanish territory, which as will be shown hereafter chiefly consist in being exempted from military jurisdiction, and being tried by civil courts, with the right to appoint advocates and solicitors and other agents, having free access to be present at the proceedings and at the taking of all the examinations and evidence which may be exhibited in the trial.

Mr. Williams called, early in the morning of Monday, the 25th of February, 1895, on the Governor-General, represented to him verbally all that was proper and pertinent in regard to the matter, and announced that some time in the same day, or the following, he would submit his representations in writing. The Governor-General who, as Mr. Williams says (despatch of March 23, 1895, printed in Document No. 104, Senate, 54th Congress, 2nd Session, page 7), "was surprised on learning the fact of the American citizenship of Sanguily having been recognized by the Governments of the United States and Spain," received his information with unmistakable signs of displeasure. It appears from a despatch of May 6th, 1895, printed on page 13 and the following of the Document above quoted, that the Governor-General answered Mr. Williams "in an outburst of most violent language and gesture, saying that it was a disgrace to the American flag for the Government of the United States to protect these men, who, it was notoriously known, were conspirators against the Government of Spain, and in still more violent language and gesture that American citizens were openly conspiring in the United States against Spain, and that he would shoot every one caught with arms in hand in any attempt against the Government of the Island, regardless of the consequences."

Such an exhibition of temper which was repeated in subsequent interviews held between Mr. Williams and Governor-General Calleja, on February 27th and March 2d, 1895, accompanied by threats, more or less openly made, that Mr. William's *exequatur* would be withdrawn, or that the Washington Government would be requested to remove him, — although highly improper in an official of his rank, and rather unusual in a man, who personally was never accused, even by his bitterest political enemies, except of being too lenient and considerate,—did not prevent the communication of the United States Consul-General from being received and given due attention.

The idea of Governor-General Calleja was that through the interposition of the United States Consul-General in favor of

Sanguily, Aguirre, Carrillo and others, the authority he had assumed for dealing with a situation which he deemed to be critical was snatched from his hands. And as he thought, right or wrong, that that authority was necessary to save the situation, he at first was angered by the sudden obstacle which sprung up before him, and then tried to overcome it. (*)

The first answer in writing which Mr. Williams received in regard to the case of Julio Sanguily was dated on March 1st, 1895, and it was to the effect that before extending to the pris-

---

(*) The explanation which Governor Calleja himself gave of this incident, in the Spanish Senate, on July 4th, 1896, is characteristic, and may be read with interest:

"As soon as I got rid of 'legal restrictions' (*trabas legales*),—when in view of the incoming imminent rebellion I had decided upon my own exclusive responsibility to place the Island under martial law and cause the Law of Public Order to be put into operation ;—when scarcely I had begun to enjoy the freedom of action which this Law permits, to use such means as I deemed conducive to save the threatened interests of the country, and to cause the arrest to be made of the most prominent leaders of the movement, among them *three of the greatest experience, importance and prestige*, who were to place themselves at the head of the insurgents in Havana, Las Villas and Matanzas ; when scarcely I had succeeded in securing the incarceration of Sanguily and Aguirre at the fortresses of *La Cabaña* and *El Morro*, and of Carrillo at the Volunteers Barracks at Remedios ;—just at the moment in which these measures became known to the public, which applauded them, because it was self-evident that without those three leaders the revolution could not succeed in rooting itself or having any organization at all in the Central and Western districts of the Island ;—the United States Consul General suddenly made his appearance at the door of my office, and claimed in favor of those three conspirators the benefits and privileges of the protocol of 1877.

"I cannot conceal from the Senate that I had to make a great effort to refrain at that moment, owing to the exigencies of my official position, the impulses of my mind, which impelled me to allow my indignation to burst out, for the contrariousness and deception which a claim of that nature, made at that moment, and in favor of these particular individuals had made me experience. But the claim, however irritating, was well founded, and I was forced to respect the protocol of 1877, which under express Royal Order had to be respected. The only thing I could do, was to use a dilatory plea, and demand the proof that those three men had complied with the registration provisions of the Law on Aliens, etc., etc."

oner the privileges of the treaty, proper evidence had to be given of his registration as a citizen of the United States of America, in the books kept to that effect in the office of the Secretary of the Governor-General.

Mr. Williams could furnish this evidence on March 4th, following, and the Governor-General had then to yield. The letter which his Secretary, Señor Don Estanislao de Antonio, wrote to Mr. Williams, on March 16th, acknowledges the fact that Julio Sanguily was a citizen of the United States of America, and explains that his case had been ordered to be transferred from the military to the civil jurisdiction, and that instructions had been given to the Judge Advocate entrusted by the Captain-General with the investigation of the charges made against the prisoner, to inhibit himself from the cognizance of the case in favor of the civil authority.

The action of Mr. Williams was declared by the State Department, March 11th, 1895, to be correct and proper, and was approved.

In view of these facts, the accusation often made, in this case, as well as in others, in newspapers and elsewhere, that Mr. Williams was slow and reluctant in the fulfillment of his duties, as far as protecting American citizens was concerned, and that the administration of Mr. Cleveland, with Mr. Olney, Secretary of State, allowed American citizens to be deprived by Spain of their treaty rights, ignominiously falls to the ground. All that properly could be done in this line was instantly done and done with success.

## III

### THE KIDNAPPING COMPLICATION.

Just at the moment in which these things were happening, and the transfer of Julio Sanguily from military to civil jurisdiction had been secured, a complication of the most troublesome character presented itself.

It had happened that a man of high standing in Cuba, by the name of Don Antonio Fernandez de Castro, had been kidnapped by a bandit and released upon the payment of fifteen thousand dollars. The investigation of that scandalous affair had been entrusted, under the law usual in such cases and for such offenses, to a military Judge Instructor, who had found, or thought to have found, that the perpetrator of that crime, the bandit Manuel Garcia, who called himself "The King of the rural districts" (*El Rey de los Campos*) and had terrorized the country for a period of considerable extent, had been in correspondence with the leaders of the "Cuban Revolutionary Party" in New York, and received from them a commission as Colonel in the Cuban Liberating Army. The money paid for the ransom of Señor Fernandez de Castro was to go, it was stated, partly to the bandit himself, and partly to the Cuban revolutionary agents to buy arms and ammunition.

It is not shown very clearly upon what ground the suspicion arose that Sanguily was connected, not of course with the kidnapping transaction itself, or with any personal association with Manuel Garcia, but with the disposition of that portion of the ransom's money which was to go to the benefit of the insurgent cause. A man named Don Gerardo Portela, who had been arrested as an accomplice of the bandit Garcia, was supposed to have been in relation with Sanguily concerning that matter, and upon that supposition, more or less groundless, the investigation branched out so as to ascertain to what extent, if at all, the prisoner was guilty of that additional offense.

This was the reason why the Judge Advocate who was conducting the kidnapping case, —a case entirely independent from the one for "rebellion,"—directed Sanguily to be retained in prison, at his disposal also, to await his action in the new affair.

Such an unexpected complication brought again to his feet the United States Consul-General at Havana. The right and privilege of an American citizen not to be subject, while in the dominions of Spain, to military jurisdiction, is as much vested in him when the offense with which he is charged is political, as when it is not. In this kidnapping affair Sanguily was as much beyond the jurisdiction of the Judge Advocate as he was in the case for alleged "rebellion." And upon this ground Mr. Williams promptly based his protest.

This additional holding of Julio Sanguily took place on April 25th, 1895, and twenty-four hours afterwards, Mr. Williams had already communicated with the Governor-General, and made the request that this new case, if continued, should be transferred like the other to the ordinary jurisdiction of a civil court.

At the date of this letter of Mr. Williams, April 25th, 1895, General Calleja had ceased to be the Governor-General of the Island, and had been succeeded by Marshall Don Arsenio Martinez Campos. But as this distinguished personage, after landing, not at Havana but at Santiago de Cuba, on the 19th of April, had taken the field immediately and entrusted the executive functions, at the capital of the Island, to General Don José Arderius, the *Segundo Cabo*, or Second Chief, it befell on the latter in his capacity of Acting Governor-General, to answer Mr. Williams' communication. And he did so directly, by official letter of May 7th, 1895, in which he explained the real nature of the action taken by the Judge-Advocate who was in charge of the kidnapping case, and informed Mr. Williams that on the 4th of the same month he had ordered the new case to be transferred, like the old one, from military to civil jurisdiction, and that the Judge-Advocate who was conducting the investigation had been instructed to discontinue it, in so far as Sanguily was concerned, and to cause a copy to be made of all the papers and records, or of the part thereof which referred to Sanguily, to be forwarded to the civil court.

This decision of Acting Governor-General Arderius, while in strict compliance with the wishes of the United States Consul-General and with the provisions of the treaty, improved only *pro forma* the condition of Sanguily. He continued to be held on two different charges, subject to two different trials conducted by two different civil courts, and compelled to await two sentences. And this situation was serious, because the new case practically operated at all times as an obstruction for the prompt disposition of the old one and prevented Sanguily more than once from being set at liberty.

All the efforts of Sanguily's lawyers, in the political case, to secure the release of their client, either on bail, or through the application of a kind of amnesty which Governor-General Calleja had granted three days after Sanguily's imprisonment, or through personal favor of the Governor-General (*) or otherwise, stumbled invincibly against the rock of the kidnapping case, and failed invariably.

If the whole thing was planned, as some expressions of General Calleja furnished ground to think, for the deliberate purpose of keeping Sanguily in a safe place, and preventing him

---

(*) There is evidence of undisputable character, in the possession of Mr. Sanguily, that Governor-General Calleja himself had twice made up his mind to set the prisoner at liberty. It appears, nevertheless, from independent sources, that this intention was not carried into effect the first time, owing to the rumor, whether founded or unfounded, which had reached the ears of the Governor-General, that a noisy demonstration was being prepared by the friends of the prisoner to celebrate his liberation, a part of the program having been to parade Sanguily in the streets of Havana, with a band of music at the head of the procession ;—and the second time, because of the pendency of the kidnapping case.

Marshal Martinez Campos was also highly inclined to release Sanguily. The latter feels sure, and felt so all the time, that if he had succeeded in having an interview with that distinguished personage, who honored him with his friendship, he would have been released. Sanguily wrote to him once or twice, asking him to come and see him at his cell in Fortress *La Cabaña*, but he had no answer. He sent for Marshal Martinez Campos' son, the Duke de la Seo de Urgel, who was also his friend, and he at once came to see him. Sanguily urged him to induce his father to call upon him, and he said that he would try. But Marshal Martinez Campos was afraid of himself and never came. He said more than once : "If I see 'that boy' I would not be able to overcome the temptation of letting him out of the castle."

when free from going and joining the insurgents, as Aguirre and Carrillo did, the fact must be acknowledged that the plan was successful.

During the course of the debate which took place in the Spanish Senate, on July 4th, 1896, and has been previously referred to, General Calleja expressed himself as follows: "When I ceased to be the Chief Commander in Cuba, the question that the treaty should be complied with in regard to Sanguily and Aguirre, imprisoned respectively at *La Cabaña* Fortress, and the *Morro* Castle, and that the proceedings against them should be transferred to the ordinary jurisdiction, had been decided. *I had taken nevertheless my precautions to protract the proceedings as long as possible.* I surrendered my office, and I do not know what has afterwards happened." Señor Batanero, another Senator, suggested then that all the prisoners thus benefitted by the treaty, had gone to join the insurgents.—And to this General Calleja replied:—"As far as Sanguily is concerned, he is still in prison; but if he did not go like the others to join the insurgents, *it was because I had found out some way of having him mixed up in a cause for clandestine introduction and sale of arms to the enemy, in which many persons were complicated.*"

This cause was probably no other than the one for the kidnapping of Don Antonio Fernandez de Castro, or better to say the incident thereof relating to the purchase of arms with the money paid by him for his ransom, in which as explained by Consul-General Williams' telegram of March 30th, 1896, to Mr. Rockhill, Assistant Secretary of State, there were some twenty persons in addition to Mr. Sanguily charged with participation of some kind in that business.

The kidnapping proceedings were quashed by the Court-martial in regard to all the defendants subject to its jurisdiction, on or before March 30th, 1896, when Mr. Williams telegraphed as above stated, and by the civil court, in regard to Sanguily, on April 23d following. (Telegram of Mr. Williams to Mr. Rockhill, April 24th, 1896.)

The fact that this result was not obtained until such a late date, when Sanguily had already received his first sentence,— December 2nd, 1895, in the case for rebellion,—and when this case had been taken on a writ of error to the Supreme Court at Madrid, shows how efficient *the way found out* by General Calleja to prevent Sanguily from being released, practically proved to be. "If the sentence is repealed," General Calleja said, "it is clear that Sanguily will go and join his companions." (*)

---

(*) Here is the official record of this portion of the debate, as set forth in the *Extracto Oficial*, Session of the Spanish Senate, July 4, 1896, No. 42, pages 5 and 6:—

EL GENERAL CALLEJA. Al cesar yo en el mando dejé prejuzgada la cuestión de que se cumpliera el tratado con respecto á Sanguily y Aguirre, *presos en el Morro y en la Cabaña*, pasando los procedimientos á la jurisdicción ordinaria. Sin embargo de que *yo había tomado mis precauciones* para dilatar todo lo posible el procedimiento. Entregué el mando, é ignoro lo ocurrido después.

EL SEÑOR BATANERO. Están todos al frente de sus partidas.

EL GENERAL CALLEJA. Todos, no; pero puede colegirse lo occurrido, porque he leido repetidas veces en los periódicos que Aguirre y Carrillo están en la manigua al frente de dos importantes partidas insurrectas.

EL SEÑOR ABARZUZA. Sea de ello lo que quiera, *nosotros los dejamos presos.*

EL GENERAL CALLEJA. En cuanto á Sanguily está preso; pero *si no se marchó también, fué porque yo hallé medio* de que quedara *encartado* en una causa en que había muchos complicados, por introducción clandestina y venta de armas al enemigo; fué sentenciado, y creo que pende del Tribunal Supremo el recurso de casación de la sentencia dictada por la Audiencia de la Habana ; y claro está que *si la sentencia se casa*, Sanguily *se irá con sus compañeros.*

(TRANSLATION.)

GENERAL CALLEJA. When I transmitted to my successor the command of the Island, the question, whether the treaty (the Cushing-Calderon-Collantes Protocol of 1877) was or was not to be complied with in regard to Sanguily and Aguirre, imprisoned respectively in the *Morro*

It is not by any means a new thing for law and reason to be silent in times of war—*silent enim leges inter arma.* But this trumped up business, which bothered Sanguily from April 25, 1895, to April 26, 1896, seems to have exceeded the limits of endurance. Judging from all the appearances the Spanish authorities themselves felt ashamed of it.

---

*Castle* and *Fortress La Cabaña,* had been settled, and the proceedings against them had been transferred to the ordinary courts; *but I had taken* my precautions for securing the delay of said proceedings as much as possible. After I surrendered the command, I do not know what happened.

SENOR BATANERO. All the prisoners are now with the insurgents.

GENERAL CALLEJA. Not all; but, judging from what has happened, it is easy to suppose what would have happened also with Sanguily—I have read in the newspapers that Aguirre and Carillo are now at the head of two important bands of insurgents.

SEÑOR ABAZUZA. The fact is that we left them all in prison.

GENERAL CALLEJA. As to Sanguily, I will say that if he did not go with the others to the insurgent camp, it was because I found out a way to mix him up in a cause for clandestine importation of arms and the sale thereof to the enemy in which many persons were complicated. The Audiencia of Havana has passed a sentence against him, which now pends before the Supreme Court here on a writ of error. It is clear that if the sentence of the Audiencia of Havana is repealed, Sanguily will go to the field with his companions.

## IV

### THE TREATY RIGHTS OF AMERICAN CITIZENS WHEN TRIED IN SPANISH TERRITORY.

Article VII of the treaty between the United States and Spain, signed at San Lorenzo el Real, on October 27th, 1795, and proclaimed after due ratification and exchange on August 2nd, 1796, contains the following provision:

"and in all cases of seizure, detention, or arrest, for debts contracted, or offenses committed by any citizen or subject of the one party within the jurisdiction of the other, the same shall be made and prosecuted by order and authority of law only, and according to the regular course of proceeding usual in such cases. The citizens and subjects of both parties shall be allowed to employ such advocates, solicitors, notaries, agents and factors as they may judge proper, in all their affairs, and in all their trials at law, in which they may be concerned, before the tribunals of the other party; and such agents shall have free access to be present at the proceedings in such causes, and at the taking of all examinations and evidence which may be exhibited in the said trials."

Among the papers sent by Mr. Pinckney, the American negotiator of that treaty, together with the treaty itself, to Mr. Randolph, the United States Secretary of State, October 28, 1795, there is a memorandum explanatory of each article of the compact (American State Papers, Foreign Relations, Vol. I, page 545) which, in respect to this Article VII, reads as follows:

"Art. 7. The first part taken from the 16th of Prussia; the latter part I added because I considered it a good stipulation in all situations, but particularly so in Spain."

Mr. Pinckney alluded probably to the methods of the Inquisition and of other Spanish tribunals having criminal jurisdiction, where the secrecy of the proceedings was carried to the utmost extremity, where torture was resorted to as a means of investigation, and where the defense of the prisoners was minimized and actually reduced in most cases to a mere *pro forma* transaction. But he scarcely could have formed such a complete idea of the correctness of his judgment in deeming said last part of the provision to be good, as subsequent events, specially in the Island of Cuba, have fully demonstrated.

Cuba and Spain had gone together, running always the same fate politically, until the moment, sadly to be remembered by Cuba, in which Spain, terrorized by the loss of her sovereignty over Mexico, Central America and the whole of South America, outside of Brazil, decided to treat Cuba as if she were an enemy, placing her perpetually under martial law, and subjecting her in all things to the autocratic rule of a Military Commander. Spain believed that in this way she could prevent Cuba from following the example of the other Spanish colonies and proclaiming and securing her independence.

That decision of Spain was carried out by means of two steps of great significance. *First*, the Royal Order of May 28th, 1825, which was the Public Law of Cuba between that date and February 10th, 1878, when the compromise which ended the war of 1868–1878 was agreed upon. And *second*, the establishment in Havana, on March 4th of the same year, 1825, of a "Permanent and Executive Military Commission," with competent jurisdiction to take cognizance of all political cases and of many other cases.

Under the Royal Order of May 28th, 1825, the Governors General of Cuba were given the same powers as belong in time of war to the governors of places besieged by an enemy.(*)

------

(*)This Royal Order reads as follows : "His Majesty being fully persuaded that at no time and under no circumstances whatever is there any possibility of weakening the principles of rectitude and love to his royal person which characterize your excellency, and His Majesty being desirous at the same time to guard against the difficulties which might arise in extraordinary cases from a division of commands, and from the complexity of powers and attributions in the respective public authorities, and with the important object of maintaining in your most precious island his legitimate sovereign authority as well as preserving public tranquility, has been graciously pleased in conformity with the advice of his council of State, to give your excellency full unrestricted power, conferring upon you all the faculties which by the royal ordinances are granted to the gover-

And under the Royal Order which established the Military Commission as a permanent tribunal, the proceedings of the so-called trials for offenses subject to the jurisdiction of the latter, ceased to be conducted in the ordinary way of law, and became secret, at least in the most important stages, full of restrictions as to the rights of the prisoners and their defense, and always hasty.

The first conflict, or at least the first serious one, which arose between the United States and Spain out of this peculiar condition of things in the Island of Cuba, was caused by the trial and condemnation by the Military Commission in 1851, of a

---

nors of cities besieged by an enemy. In consequence of this His Majesty gives your excellency ample and unlimited authorization, not merely to eject from the island and send to the peninsula any public functionaries, whatever may be their office, rank, class or condition, whose stay in the island may be prejudicial, or whose public or private conduct may arouse your suspicion, and replace them temporarily by such faithful servants of His Majesty as may merit all your excellency's confidence, but also to suspend the execution of any orders or general instructions whatever, emanating from any of the Departments of the Government, in such degree as your excellency may deem expedient for the royal service, such suspensions being in all cases provisional, and your excellency being required to give account thereof to His Majesty. In extending to your excellency this signal proof of his royal appreciation and of the high confidence he reposes in your well-known loyalty, His Majesty hopes that in worthy justification of this confidence you will display the greatest prudence and circumspection, and the most untiring activity, and trusts that your excellency, being by this present act of his royal bounty placed under a most rigid responsibility, will cause the laws to be observed, justice to be administered, and the faithful vassals of His Majesty to be protected and rewarded, and secure, furthermore, without hesitation or dissimulation the punishment of those who, forgetful of their obligations and of what they owe to the best and most beneficent of sovereigns, would violate their duties and give free rein to their criminal machinations against the laws and the established system of government.

By royal order I communicate this to your excellency for your information.

May God preserve your excellency many years.

MADRID, *May* 28, 1825.

AYMERICH.

The CAPTAIN-GENERAL *of the Island of Cuba.*

citizen of the United States of America, residing in Havana. Mr. John S. Trasher, a native of the State of Maine, tried at Havana "for the crime of treason" and condemned to imprisonment for six years at hard labor in the penitentiary at Ceuta, in Africa, protested against his having been subjected to military jurisdiction and tried by court-martial under rules of military procedure, all in violation of his rights and privileges as secured by the provisions of Article VII of the treaty; and his protest was supported by the United States Government.

But, as shown by Document No. 10, House of Representatives, 32d Congress, 1st Session, the Captain General of Cuba, then General Don José de la Concha, made the point against the said protest that Mr. Trasher had been tried exactly in the same manner as was provided by the treaty. The latter said that the trial should be conducted "according to the regular course of proceeding usual in such cases," and in Cuba there was no other regular and usual course of proceeding applicable to Mr. Trasher's case than the proceeding of the Military Commission. General Concha said: "The Military Commission established in this Island since the year 1825 is a common and ordinary tribunal for the trial of such crimes as are committed against the State. It was therefore the only authority competent to pass sentence upon Mr. Trasher, who stood accused of conspiracy, and he (Mr. Trasher) could not have been tried by any other tribunal without manifest violation of the laws by which we are governed." (General Concha to Minister Calderón de la Barca, November 28, 1851; *Ibid.*, page 24.)

The issue was avoided and the contention closed by Spain granting a pardon to Mr. Trasher.

Two years afterwards another singular contention was started by Count Alcoy, Spanish Secretary of State, who said to Mr. Barringer, Minister of the United States at Madrid, that the treaty of 1795 was not applicable to the colonies of Spain. (Ex. Doc. No. 86, House of Representatives, 33d Congress, 1st session, page 219.) To this Mr. Barringer replied : "As to the great principle now for the first time invoked in bar to this claim, and compared with which the claim itself, though important to the petitioners, is as nothing, viz : that the treaty of 1795 was never applicable to the Spanish colonies, I cannot do less than repeat my surprise at a proposition, which a review of all the diplomatic intercourse between Spain and the United States will disclose, is of the most recent origin, which is contrary to what has ever been the understanding of the latter, and which in the opinion of the undersigned is not sustained by any examination of the provisions of the treaty itself, nor by its contemporaneous or subsequent history or construction.'' (Mr. Barringer to Count Alcoy, Madrid, March 19, 1853, page 222 *Ibid.*)

During the ten years of the Cuban war of independence of 1868-1878, many cases occurred in which the true construction of the provisions of the treaty was made the subject of serious argument and dispute. But the matter was set at rest by means of an authorative expression of opinion on the part of the Spanish government, in so far as to its own understanding of the obligations imposed on it by the treaty was concerned.

This expression of opinion was made at a conference between Mr. Caleb Cushing, United States Minister at Madrid, and Don Fernando Calderón y Collantes, Spanish Minister of State, held at Madrid, January 12th, 1877, and witnessed by a protocol which since that time has become famous.

Señor Calderón y Collantes declared that the understanding of Spain of the stipulations of Article VII of the treaty of 1795, was that '' no citizen of the United States, residing in Spain, her adjacent islands, or her ultramarine possessions, charged with acts of sedition, treason or conspiracy against the institutions, the public security, the integrity of the territory, or against the Supreme Government, or any other crime whatsoever, shall be subject to trial by any exceptional tribunal, but exclusively by the ordinary jurisdiction, except in the case of being captured with arms in hand.''

This clear and explicit statement, which no doubt constituted a great victory for the United States, as it put an end to all former Spanish contentions, secured in favor of American citizens a privilege of great value, which the further declarations of the instrument, relating to the manner and form of the proceedings to be resorted to in the above mentioned trials by ordinary civil courts, strongly corroborated. Señor Calderón y Collantes said that such proceedings should be the ones provided for by the Law of April 17th, 1821, which although repealed in European Spain and replaced by another law called of Public Order, of April 23d, 1870, was nevertheless at that time the law in force in Cuba (*).

Mr. Cushing in his note to Mr. Fish, Secretary of State, of February 4th, 1877 (Foreign Relations of the United States in 1877, page 494), recognized that this law contained "tyrannical features, of which Spain herself had had sad experience ; " and he was right in expressing himself in this way, because that law of 1821, called by all in Spain *La Ley Marcial,* " The Martial Law," enacted by the liberals to tyrannize the partisans of absolute monarchy, had been held in abhorrence on account of its extreme severity since the days of its promulgation. Its application to Cuba by Royal Decree of March 28th, 1866, was due to no other thing than its cruelty and the expeditious way which its provisions furnished to deal with life and property. This law, however, and its methods of procedure were repealed by the Penal Code of Spain which was made applicable to Cuba on July 11th, 1879, and by the Rules for the enforcement of the provisions of the same code, enacted May 23d, 1879. From the day of the promulgation of this new law, a new condition of things, much more liberal perhaps in this respect than in any other country in the world was created in Cuba ; and this fact must never be forgotten, if the true spirit of the protocol of 1877, rather than its letter, is to be attended to.

(*) The Law of Public Order was not promulgated in Cuba until the 24th of September, 1879.

And it was for this reason that such an expert diplomatist as Mr. John W. Foster, when negotiating with Spain the treaty of commerce, of November 18th, 1884, which was not ratified by the Senate of the United States, made an effort to secure and secured from Spain the following provision :

"Article XX. The citizens of the United States in the Islands of Cuba and Puerto Rico, and reciprocally the Spanish subjects in the United States, shall enjoy for their professions, industries and business of whatever character, whether individually, in the quality of associates, or in a co-operative capacity, the same privileges which the citizens of the territory of their residence enjoy, on condition, however, of their being subject to the laws of the country in which they reside. They shall also have free and easy access to the tribunals of justice to maintain their suits and defend their rights and claims, and the high contracting parties ratify by the present treaty the principles and provisions set forth in the protocol signed at Madrid on the 12th of January, 1877; it being understood that it shall be applied in all its effects to cases in which the accused are not more favored in respect to their defense and rights by the law for the application of the Penal Code in the Island of Cuba promulgated on the 23d of May, 1879, and that it shall be applied in the same manner provided, when they are subject to military jurisdiction in virtue of the stipulation of said protocol hereby ratified."

The truth is that such a choice between the two laws, namely the Law of 1821 and the Penal Code and the Law for its application of 1879, is now, and has been for some time, entirely unnecessary. The Law of 1821 became obsolete both in regard to prisoners taken with arms in hand, to be tried by military courts, according to military proceedings, and in regard to prisoners otherwise captured, to be tried by courts of ordinary jurisdiction, according to civil proceedings. And the fact that it became so obsolete, and that it was replaced *in toto* as to people captured with arms in hands by the Law of Public Order of April 23d, 1870, and as to people captured otherwise by the Penal Code and the Law for the application thereof of 1879, is certainly to be deemed a great benefit.

None of the "tyrannical features," referred to by Mr.

Cushing, of the Law of 1821 can be found in the new laws which have superseded it. Even the so-called *Council of War*, which takes cognizance of the cases of prisoners captured with arms in hand, can hardly be considered a real court martial. (*) As to the proceedings according to which the ordinary prosecutions have to be conducted against prisoners captured otherwise, it is necessary to recognize that they are marked by great consideration of the rights of the defendants.

While, for instance, under Article 32 of the Law of 1821, the sentences of death are to be executed "within forty-eight hours and the others in the shortest possible time," under the Rules for the application of the Penal Code (Rule 79) in case of death penalty, an appeal to the Supreme Court of Madrid is always understood to be taken by the prisoner. Said appeal may also be taken, although only under certain rules, against all other sentences.

Under the law of 1821 no petitions for pardon can be admitted or considered (Art. 33); but under the new laws no restriction exists as to applications for clemency.

Judging from some statements made in the Senate and elsewhere, during the public discussion of the Sanguily case, the idea seems to have prevailed, that the true, genuine privilege of citizens of the United States of America, when tried in Spanish territory, is to be tried according to the course of proceeding established by the Law of April 17, 1821; and on this ground, for instance, complaints were made because Sanguily was tried by a Court consisting of five members, and not by a Court consisting of six members, as required by Article 28 of the said Law of 1821. But all of this was said and argued without notice having been taken that the judicial machinery

---

(*)Article 29 of of the Law of Public Order provides as follows : "This Council of War shall consist of four Captains of the Army appointed by the Military authority, of one Judge of first instance, of one Justice of the Peace, and of the District Attorney. If the Justice of the Peace selected is not a lawyer, he shall be replaced by another Justice of the Peace learned in the law, and if none is found the senior practicing lawyer of the locality where the Council is held, will fill his place"

of the law of 1821 is not the judicial machinery, immensely superior, of the present date, and that it was better for the prisoner to be tried by five judges, with the right to appeal to the Supreme Court of Spain, which he used twice, than to be tried by six judges, whose decision was final.

The grand point which was gained for American citizens, in so far as the interpretation of Article VII of the treaty of 1795 is concerned, consists in the fact that under no circumstances, and in all parts of the Spanish dominions, their trials for all kinds of offenses have to be conducted exclusively by ordinary jurisdiction, except only in case that they are captured with arms in hand,—and furthermore that they have the right to appoint lawyers or agents to whom free access has to be given to be present at all the stages of the proceedings, and at the taking of all examinations and evidence which may be made and used in the said trials.

This is the essential point, which always has excited to the highest degree the anger of the Captains-General. Whatever may be alleged against the Cushing-Calderón y Collantes Protocol of 1877, the fact remains that by the action of the Spanish Government, the Spanish declaration contained in it was made part and parcel of the Spanish Law, because that declaration of the opinion of Señor Calderón y Collantes as to the real meaning of Article VII of the treaty of 1795, was sanctioned by the King of Spain, and embodied in a Royal Order, which was officially communicated to the Governor-General of Cuba, with peremptory instructions to comply with it. And it is for this reason that General Calleja said that he could not help himself against the Protocol, and that he had to obey the Royal Order, no matter how unpalatable, which referred to it.

All the other things contained in the protocol are changeable and of secondary character, and they must be considered in relation to the greatest benefit of the prisoner and to nothing else. The real and proper criterion to be used in these matters is the one which was used by the State Department, when instructing the United States Consul General at Havana, November 9th, 1895, in regard to Sanguily's case. It is clear for instance, that prisoners have a right to demand a speedy trial ; but circumstances may arise in which the interests of the prisoner will be better subserved by securing delay. If upon the arrival of those circumstances the counsel does not make all that is in his power to secure that delay, he may find out very soon that he made a mistake. Instead of "defending" his client and endeavoring to save him, he may have aided perhaps to secure his conviction.

When Assistant Secretary of State, Mr. Uhl, instructed United States Consul-General Williams, November 9th, 1895, to be in frequent consultation with Sanguily's lawyer, to confer with him freely, and to endeavor to avoid as well unseemly haste to Sanguily's disfavor as prolonged delays to his injury, he did the very best that could be legally done in this respect.

## V

### THE TRIAL.

Between the 16th of March, 1895, at which date the Governor-General decided to instruct the Judge Advocate who was investigating the charge of "rebellion" against Sanguily to inhibit himself from the cognizance of the case in favor of the civil authority, and the 28th of November of the same year, at which date the trial of the prisoner commenced, fully eight months had elapsed. The record does not show why such an extraordinary delay took place, nor does it in any way remove the apprehension that it was unwarranted and exclusively due to the idea, which seems to have prevailed in this affair from the beginning to the end, that it was better for Spain to keep Sanguily within the walls of a fortress than give him an opportunity to go away and join the insurgents.

Assistant Secretary of State, Mr. Edwin F. Uhl, had sent a telegram to Mr. Springer, Acting Consul General at Havana, under date of June 18th, 1895, instructing him to demand that Sanguily would be given speedily civil trial, or else released; and Assistant Secretary of State, Mr. Alvey A. Adee, on September 3d, 1895, had repeated the instruction, and said to Mr. Williams by cable, that "the Department felt compelled to demand (Sanguily's) immediate trial or release."

Marshal Martinez Campos, who was no less reluctant than his predecessor and all other Spanish Generals and military officials to be restricted, when dealing with American citizens, on account of the treaty, raised at once a question, which was promising at least of long diplomatic discussion and therefore of long delay. In replying to Mr. Williams he stated that " Consuls are not vested with diplomatic functions, and cannot rightfully present any official remonstrations in government affairs,"—that they could only be allowed to address the authorities confidentially for the purpose of inquiring into facts and reporting to their repective governments,—that he, the Governor General himself, had no authority to deal with international questions,—and that whatever the United States Government might be willing to say on the subject had to be said in Madrid to the Spanish Minister of State (*).

This official communication dated September 6th, three days subsequent to Mr. Adee's telegram to Mr. Williams, was accompanied by a personal letter of the same date, wherein Marshal Martinez Campos called Mr. Williams " My dear Sir and Friend," and in which he said that he took pleasure *in personally informing* Mr. Williams that Sanguily's case *will soon be heard.*

The record shows that on the 9th of November, 1895, Assistant Secretary of State, Mr. Edwin F. Uhl, said to Consul-General Williams, among other things, what follows:—

---

(*) The discussion of the question thus raised about the right of the United States Consul General at Havana to present remonstrances,—a question which was settled favorably to the United States, on October 23d, 1895, can be found from page 8 to page 13 of Document No. 224, House of Representatives, 54th Congress, 1st session.

" This Government has continuously asserted the right of Mr. Sanguily, as a citizen of the United States, to be tried on formulated charges by the ordinary resorts stipulated by the treaty of 1795 and by the protocol of 1877. This demand has been acceded to, and while the proceedings have been marked with what from our point of view appears to be extraordinary tardiness, I am not advised that there has been a tangible denial of justice in the case. It is due, however, to Mr. Sanguily himself, as well as to the Government which has necessarily intervened for his protection, that he should be accorded as speedy a trial as may be consistent with his own interests and with the necessary opportunity for full examination of the charges and preparation of his defense. You are presumed to be in consultation with Mr. Sanguily's advocate, and should confer freely with him on this point, endeavoring to avoid as well unseemly haste to his disfavor as prolonged delays to his injury."

The trial began as has been said on the 28th of November, 1895, at 12 o'clock M. The Government was represented by the *Fiscal* or Prosecuting Attorney, Señor Don Federico Enjuto, and the prisoner by Don Miguel F. Viondi, a member of the bar at Havana. The tribunal consisted of five Judges, as follows : Señor Don José Pulido, Presiding Judge, Señor Don Francisco Pampillón, Señor Don Vicente Pardo Bonanza, Señor Don Adolfo Astudillo de Guzmán, and Señor Don Rafael Maydagán, Associate Judges.

The United States Consul-General was instructed by the State Department, November 14th, 1895, to attend the trial as spectator, and make concise but sufficient report of the proceedings.

The prosecution made an effort to poison the mind of the Court against the prisoner by referring at length and with as much force as was at its command, to the political ideas of the prisoner and his former affiliations, his services to the cause of the independence of Cuba during the war of 1868–1878, and his abjuration of his Spanish allegiance and his naturalization in the United States, in the latter year. But as far as the specific charge upon which the prisoner was on trial, the prosecution did not produce more evidence than the same so-called one which had been secured by it in violation of the treaty during the period of military investigation.

That evidence was clearly inadmissible, and ought to have been stricken out or rejected. Assistant Secretary of State, Mr. Edwin F. Uhl, in his dispatch to Mr. Williams, of December 23d, 1895, expressed, with reason, the apprehension that such a method of proceedings against Sanguily "was not in accordance with the treaty of 1795, as construed by the protocol of 1877," because as shown by the record the civil court had merely taken up the case where the military tribunal had left it off, the trial being based and conducted upon the same charges formulated, and upon the evidence taken by the Judge Advocate. This undue continuation, and attempted revalidation of proceedings taken in violation of a law of such a high character and supremacy as an international compact is, and by authorities which under the same compact had no competent jurisdiction to take them, was a practical nullification of the treaty privileges of the prisoner.

This inadmissible and improper so-called evidence, upon which the prosecution succeeded, however, in securing the conviction of Sanguily was substantially as follows:

I. An affidavit or certified statement of Governor-General Calleja, dated March 25, 1895 (see pages 8 and 9), stating nothing on the affiant's own personal knowledge, but merely on information acquired through confidential communications and reports, which were never produced.

II. A number of papers purporting to be copies of letters alleged to have been written by Sanguily at Havana, at various times previous to February 23d, 1895, and addressed to Don José Martí and some other individuals residing in New York and other cities of the United States of America. It was explained that the originals of the said letters, as well as the originals of other letters mailed at Havana to the same addresses, had been detained at the Havana Post Office, and opened, and read and copied, and thereafter resealed and forwarded to their respective destinations, and that copies thus obtained had been sent to the Governor-General, and by him to the Judge Advocate, to be made a part of the record.

It is hardly necessary to suggest that such so-called copies, alleged to have been obtained through a process so highly disreputable and so much to be condemned, especially when resorted to before the constitutional guarantees were suspended, ought not to have been admitted in evidence.

As the prisoner denied to have written the letters whose alleged copies were shown to him, it seems to be clear that the production thereof as proofs only served to show the bad behavior of the postal authorities of Cuba in tampering with the mails of the Postal Union, and also the clumsy way of their tampering.

III. A letter which together with some other papers of no value was found by the police in a drawer of a cupboard, in a room which Sanguily had occupied in a house on the estate called *Portela*, in the rural district of Aguacate. Said letter, which has no address, but was claimed by the prosecution to have been written to Sanguily, contains a passage which translated into English reads as follows: "None better than you, for your respectable surroundings, the credit which your name will impart to the movement, your old and well-established reputation as a revolutionist and a soldier, and the position which you have always occupied amidst both parties, is called to lead a serious and important movement."

This letter, which the prisoner did not recognize, and which no person can say who wrote it or to whom it was addressed, might at all events be construed as an invitation from the writer to the man to whom it was sent to join the rebellion ; but it never can be taken as an acceptance of the invitation or a proof of the actual joining, or attempting to join, the movement to which it refers.

IV. A paper, or better to say the fragments of a paper, torn to pieces and chewed up by a man named Don José Inocencio Azcuy, in whose possession it was found when he was arrested by the police at the moment he landed in Havana, coming from Key West, Florida, said fragments having been more or less illegibly arranged, and made a part of the record.*

The prosecution claimed that this paper, which has no date, was an original commission of Colonel in the insurgent army issued by Sanguily, as chief commander of the same, in favor of Azcuy.

Sanguily denied to have ever seen that paper or written it, or to know Mr. Azcuy, or have ever heard of him or of the said commission.

V. The deposition of Señor Trujillo, a Police Inspector, who said that he arrested Don José Inocencio Azcuy, on his landing from a steamer from Key West, that he searched him and untied his cravat; that inside the said cravat he found the paper referred to in the foregoing paragraph; that Azcuy by a sudden move-

---

(*)The text of this strange document, as arranged by the prosecution, and on file, is as follows :

" Sr. D. J. Azu—Coronel del Ejer—ciudadano—competentemente autor—Coronel de nuestro—sub—y—Queda V. actor—z—conferir nombran—todas que por mi merit—cios los merezca—organizará fuerzas que—to le iran a U.—instrucciones—sobre la manera ó—ganiz—los y puntos que ha de ocupar—confiamos en su celo—tico espera—zo affmo, su y P. J. S—nguily—"

A true translation into English of the foregoing text, such as it was left, after it passed through the chewing process and the struggle between Mr. Azcuy and the policeman, is a matter of great difficulty; but an idea of its meaning may be formed by the following :

" Sr. D. J. Azu—Colonel of the Arm—citizen—competently author—Colonel of our—sub—and—You are author—z—to confer appoint—all that my merit—ces deserve them—Shall organize forces which—to they will go to you—instructions—on the manner or—ganiz—them and points which you have (or he has) to occupy—We trust in your zeal—tico—expects—zo—most affectionate, your (or his) P. J. S—nguily."

ment snatched it from his (Trujillo's) hands and put it in his mouth and tried to chew it up; that he (Trujillo) engaged then in a struggle with Azcuy in order to rescue the paper, and that he succeeded with the greatest difficulty "in securing a part of it," and "taking another fragment out of Azcuy's mouth."

VI. The testimony of Don José Inocencio Azcuy, who explained how the paper was found inside his necktie, and how he had attempted to destroy it. Witness said that that paper was really a commission of Colonel in the insurgent army, issued in his favor, at his request, and sent to him by the Revolutionary Junta of New York, through his nephew, Don Nemesio Azcuy, who brought it to Key West, Fla. The witness further said that he had applied for this appointment of Colonel in the insurgent army, not because he would have ever thought of joining the insurgents, but because of his desire to protect himself and his estate, "El Rosario," from insurgent raids. He also stated that he did not know whether the signature affixed to the Commission was or was not Sanguily's.

VII. The depositions of three experts in caligraphy,—Señor Biosca, Señor Perez Madueño, and Señor Alvarez—who, upon examination of the fragments of paper purporting to be the commission aforesaid, and upon comparison of its handwriting and signature with other papers in the acknowledged genuine handwriting of the prisoner, and signed by him, said respectively as follows : Señor Biosca, that he deemed the handwriting and signature of the so-called commission to be similar to Sanguily's genuine handwriting and signature, but that he could not positively state that they were Sanguily's,—and Señors Perez Madueño and Alvarez, that the paper was wholly illegible and that they could not make any sense of it or fairly make any comparison between it and the other papers.

VIII. The deposition of Don Antonio Lopez Coloma, an insurgent leader captured by the authorities and afterward condemned to death and executed, who said, among other things, that an insurgent leader of high rank called Don Pedro Betan-

court had given him instructions to come to Havana and confer
with Sanguily and some others in regard to planning and starting a revolutionary movement; but that deponent had declined
to have any interview with Sanguily, and never had it, because
"he had heard that Sanguily disapproved the movement,"
and because deponent "never thought that Sanguily would
join the insurrection."

IX. A paper all rumpled up, partially torn, and carefully
pressed and fixed up afterwards, for preservation, by the Judge
Advocate, which purports to be a letter, dated February 9th,
1895, written by one "Gener," to one Don Pedro Betancourt,
and found not in the possession of Betancourt or of Sanguily,
but in a pocket of Don Antonio Lopez Coloma, when the Spanish troops captured him, on or about the 1st or the 2nd of
March, 1895. The prosecution claimed that the signature
"Gener" affixed to the letter was a bogus signature, and
that the letter had been written by Sanguily.

It was never explained how it came to pass that this letter
written by "Gener" to Betancourt found out its way to
the pocket of Lopez Coloma,—nor is it shown by the record
that the prosecution did ever take any step to identify the
person who had signed the said letter. The name "Gener"
is not by any means an uncommon name, especially in the
province of Matanzas, wherein Lopez Coloma was captured;—
and if the prosecution had not taken at once for granted that
Gener and Sanguily were one and the same person, some
light, as necessary in all judicial investigation, might have been
thrown into the subject.

The passage in this letter, claimed by the prosecution to
accriminate Sanguily, expresses the regret of the writer for
being so short of money as to become prevented from attempting anything. The writer explains that this impecunious
condition had forced him to pawn a machete and a revolver
which were his property; and then he goes on and urges
Betancourt to send to him, as soon as possible, the twenty-five

hundred dollars which had been promised. The communication closed with the following remark: "Cervantes saw himself without anything to eat at supper when he finished to write Don Quijote ; and I, when about to be placed at the head of a work of redemption, find myself without means, even to send my cook to the market."

X. The testimony of the Government expert in caligraphy, Señor Biosca, who compared the handwriting of the letter referred to in the foregoing paragraph with that of other genuine letters of the prisoner, and said that "he considered both handwritings similar, and thought that all these papers shown to him had been written by the same hand, although he could not positively state that they were so written."

Señor Perez Madueño and Señor Alvarez, the other experts in caligraphy, could not see the similarity which their colleague said to have found.

XI. The testimony of Don Ramón Sanchez, a pawnbroker in the city of Havana, who said "that about a year, a year and a half, or two years," Sanguily had pawned in his establishment a revolver and a machete, which were never redeemed."

XII. The deposition of Don José Paglieri, Chief of the Havana Police, who in answer to the question, "Had you any knowledge that he (Sanguily) was conspiring with Betancourt and Lopez Coloma at Matanzas?" said: "I know in a general way that an effort was being made in behalf of secession ; everybody knew that." And when asked by the Presiding Judge: "Did you know that Sanguily was going to place himself at the head of a band from Matanzas, Ibarra, or any other place?" he answered: "I did not know anything about it. I only knew that there was a conspiracy on foot." Counsel for defendant questioned then this witness about the reports which he as Chief of Police had made about Sanguily, and he answered: "A record of this must be in the Captain General's Office, since the Captain General was informed of the facts; I have no information except common reports which I am unable to prove."

Señor Viondi, as counsel for Sanguily, made a strong argument against the insinuations and so-called testimony of the prosecution. He earnestly endeavored to persuade the Court of the futility of all that had been alleged with reference to the part which Sanguily had taken in the war of 1868–1878. The movement represented by that war was different from the one now started. The origin, the nature, the tendencies, and the developments of the former were not the origin, nature, tendencies, and developments of the latter. And a man who fully approved the former and intimately connected himself with it might without inconsistency disapprove the latter, and even dislike it heartily and avoid all connection with it. The attention of the Court was also called to the fact that the expatriation from Spain and the giving up of the Spanish allegiance, were lawful acts, which Spanish subjects could lawfully perform, and that the naturalization of Sanguily in the United States of America could not thus be construed as an act of rebellion, and much less as evidence of his alleged connection with the present movement. The illegal character of the evidence and its undue admission were also discussed at length and proven beyond a doubt.

The affidavit of Governor-General Calleja, which under the express provisions of the treaty ought not to have been admitted as evidence against Sanguily(*), was confronted with the deposition of Colonel Paglieri, Chief of the Havana Police, and shown to be without force, because of the lack of proof of the assertions made in it, merely on confidential reports.

---

(*) Article VII of the treaty between the United States and Spain allows American citizens in Spain, and Spanish subjects in the United States, to appoint agents, advocates, etc., to assist them when on trial for any offense committed, or alleged to have been committed by them, and says : "and such agents shall have free access *to be present* at the proceedings in such causes, and *at the taking of all examinations and evidence* which may be exhibited in the said trials." Counsel for Sanguily was not present, nor allowed to be present, at the taking of Governor-General Calleja's affidavit.

The alleged copies of the supposed intercepted letter were proof only, if such a shameful tampering with the mails of the Postal Union was true, of the wickedness of the Spanish postal officials who perpetrated it.

The unsigned and unaddressed communication alleged to have been found at the Portela estate, and construed by the prosecution as an appeal to Sanguily to join the present insurrection, could never be considered, even if really sent to Sanguily, and received by him, as evidence that he yielded to the appeal and assented to lead the movement.

The connection of Sanguily with the Azcuy's mutilated paper, denied by Sanguily, denied by Azcuy, and denied by the experts in caligraphy, was not properly shown by the prosecution. An enemy of Sanguily, or an ultra officious Cuban patriot, anxious to improve his cause by the prestige of Sanguily's name, might easily have written Sanguily's name, if it was really written, at the foot of that paper. If the owner of the paper was seeking protection, as he said, against insurgent raids, the idea might have occurred to him that Sanguily's signature, whether genuine or spurious, at the foot of the document was perhaps more conducive than any other thing to the accomplishment of his purpose.

The failure of the prosecution to prove that the letter, supposed to have been found in Lopez Coloma's pocket, signed "Gener," and addressed to Don Pedro Betancourt, was really Sanguily's, was fully demonstrated by an affidavit of Don Pedro Betancourt himself, which the prisoner's counsel offered in evidence, but was not admitted by the Court. In that affidavit, sworn to before a Notary Public, in the city of New York, at a date subsequent to the filing by the prosecution of the letter herein referred to, and duly authenticated, Don Pedro Betancourt denied to have ever received such letter, and explained the reasons why he deemed it to be spurious.

When the prisoner himself was examined he emphatically denied to have connected himself in any way whatever with the present revolution. He said distinctly that "he was in no way concerned in the uprising and had had nothing to do with it," that he had refused to entertain any relation at all with it, and that "he had kept entirely aloof from the movement."

This positive and emphatic declaration by the prisoner was corroborated by the testimony of Lopez Coloma and others, as well as by the fact, which seems to be obvious, that if Sanguily would have been connected with the rebellion in such principal and important a manner as the prosecution claimed, he would not have remained quietly at his home twenty-four hours after the proclamation of martial law in the Island, patiently await-ing to be arrested.

The counsel for the prisoner made the additional point and made it ably, that even if Sanguily had done what the prose-cution claimed, his offense was not "rebellion," but "con-spiracy for rebellion," which is a different offense under Article 244 of the Penal Code. This offense is punishable with "correctional imprisonment," not less than six months and one day, and not more than six years, and not with imprison-ment for life at hard labor as desired by the prosecution.

An effort was made also by the same distinguished lawyer to secure for his client the application of the amnesty granted by Governor-General Calleja, three days after the imprisonment of Sanguily, and extended even to those insurgents in arms, who would be willing to surrender.

## VI.

### THE SENTENCE.

The sentence passed by the Court, as read in public by the Presiding Judge, Don José Pulido, at twenty minutes past four, P. M., of Monday, December 2nd, 1895, was as follows:

"In the City of Havana, on the 2nd of December, 1895, in the case pending before Section 3d of the Criminal Court, be-tween the Government, and Don Julio Sanguily y Garit, a native and a resident of this capital, but a citizen of the United

States of America, 44 years old, married, the son of Don Julio
Sanguily, and Doña María Garit de Sanguily, a business man
by occupation, a man of education, with no criminal record,
for the crime of rebellion,—the Government being represented
by the Prosecuting Attorney and the defendant Sanguily by
Solicitor Don Juan Plutarco Valdés and the lawyer Don Miguel
Francisco Viondi:

" 1. Whereas in the proceedings instituted by order of the
military authorities and by military justice against Don Eladio
Larrinaga, Don Julio Sanguily, Don José María Aguirre and
others, charged with the crime of ' rebellion,' it was ordered
that a certified copy of the record in so far as concerning the
aforesaid Sanguily and Aguirre should be made and turned
over to the civil authorities, because under the protocol of
January 12th, 1877, the said civil authorities are the only ones
having competent jurisdiction to try the case of the said two
prisoners, for the reason that they are citizens of the United
States of America : it appearing that the said order was complied with, and that the copy so ordered to be made and turned
over to the civil authorities was first transmitted to the Senior
Judge of this city, and by him subsequently and for the purposes of examination and prosecution to the Judge of Instruction for El Cerro district, who proceeded to prepare the case for
proper trial (*):

2. Whereas it is proved that Don Julio Sanguily y Garit,
whose affiliations with the separatist party, in which he enjoyed
influence and prestige, owing to the services which he had rendered to the rebel cause in the insurrection which ended in
1878, kept himself in relations with persons residing in this
Island and abroad for the purpose of organizing an uprising to
secure independence;—and that he was one of the abettors and
leaders of the present uprising (†) :

" 3. Whereas, it is proved that Don Antonio Lopez Coloma,
a resident of the district of Matanzas came to this capital on the
21st of February, 1895, for the purpose of receiving orders and
instructions from Don Julio Sanguily, as to whether the cry of

(*) The language of this part of the decision shows how just the remarks
of Assistant Secretary of State Mr. Uhl were when he said that Sanguily's
case had been merely taken up by the Civil authorities where the Military
authorities had left it off; and that what was done under military jurisdiction, although null and void, had been accepted and validated.

(†) This statement, merely a *petitio principii*, takes for granted and
gives as proved precisely the same fact which was to be investigated.
No legal proof was ever produced of the correspondence alluded to by
the Court in this part of the sentence.

"Long live the independence" should or should not be raised:—
that both of them agreed as to starting the revolutionary
movement on the 24th of the same month;—that the said
revolutionary movement broke out at the date agreed upon,
several bands of men rising up in arms in open hostility
towards the Government, and proclaiming the independence
of this Island;—that the said Lopez Coloma, who had joined
one of these bands and was captured by the troops of the
Government, carried about his person, when taken prisoner,
besides his arms and various papers, one letter written by
Don Julio Sanguily, dated February 9th, and addressed to
one Mr. Betancourt, who was likewise concerned in the uprising, in which letter Sanguily lamented his lack of means, and
said that he was so poor as to be unable to take the field and
redeem a machete and a revolver which he had had to pawn,
urging Betancourt to get for him as soon as possible the twenty-
five hundred dollars which he had promised him, and adding
that he had no head to think about anything of interest, as he
saw himself, just at the moment of placing himself at the head
of a work of redemption, without means even of sending his
cook to the market (*):—

"4. Whereas it is proved that at the time in which the letter
above referred to was written, Sanguily had in a pawnbroker's
office called "La Equitativa" a machete and a revolver which
he had pawned, and were sold after his arrest.†

"5. Whereas it is proved that Don Julio Sanguily was
arrested at the house in which he lived at Havana at an early
hour in the morning of February 24th, 1895, the same day on
which the uprising took place.

"6. Whereas, it is proved that when Don José Inocencio
Azcuy arrived in this port from Tampa he was arrested by an
inspector of police, who took from him a document which he
had hidden in his cravat, and that when the aforesaid Azcuy
saw that he was discovered he snatched a part of said document
out of the hands of the inspector and put it in his mouth for
the purpose of destroying it, and that the inspector compelled
him by force to spit out the pieces, and that the said document

(*)This clause of the sentence takes it for granted that Don Antonio
Lopez Coloma saw Sanguily, which both Lopez Coloma and Sanguily
denied. Nor does it pay attention to the fact that the signature of the
letter reads "Gener" and not "Sanguily."

(†) Neither the name of the pawnbroker's office was "La Equitativa,"
nor were the revolver and machete pawned or sold when the sentence
says they were. The testimony of the pawnbroker himself, Don Ramón
Sanchez, demolishes the structure built by the Court upon movable sand.

was written and signed by Don Julio Sanguily, and was a commission of colonel in the insurgent army, with power to organize troops and make appointments;

" 7. Whereas, when the order to end the preliminary examination was confirmed, the first hearing took place, and in accordance with the request therein made by the Government attorney, an order was issued to suspend the proceedings provisionally against Don José María Aguirre, one-half of the costs to be paid by him, and to commence the public trial of Don Julio Sanguily;

" 8. Whereas, the record was delivered to the Government attorney, who made an argument characterizing the offense as rebellion, as described by Article 237, No. 1, and punished in Article 238 of the Penal Code, and asked that Don Julio Sanguily y Garit should be sentenced as guilty of the aforesaid crime to imprisonment for life, with the accessory penalties of Article 33 of the Code, and to the payment of one-half of the costs;

" 9. Whereas, the counsel for the defense, in his turn, asked for the acquittal of the prisoner on the ground that there was no legal reason to suppose that his client had committed the acts attributed to him, and proposed as an alternative that his client should be pardoned on the ground that he was included in the proclamation published on the 27th day of February;

" 10. Whereas the proofs offered by the Government attorney and the prisoner's counsel having been accepted, a day was appointed for holding the public trial, on which occasion they reiterated their previous arguments;

" 11. Whereas, according to Article 8 of the Civil Code and Article 41 of the Law concerning foreigners, the penal laws are binding upon all persons living in Spanish territory, and that consequently, the provisions of the Penal Code are applicable to Don Julio Sanguily y Garit, since his American citizenship gives him only the rights granted by the protocol of January 12, 1877, which rights have been recognized;

" 12. Whereas, according to Article 237, No. 1, of the Penal Code, persons who publicly rise in arms in open hostility to the Government in order to proclaim the independence of Cuba and Puerto Rico, or of either of them, are guilty of the crime of rebellion;

" 13. Whereas the acts declared to have been proved in the third " whereas " constitute the consummated crime defined in the twelfth " whereas," since the object and purpose of the rising, which took place on the 24th of February, is to secure the independence of this Island;

" 14. Whereas, according to Article 238 of the same code,

persons who induce others to become rebels by promoting or sustaining the rebellion, and the principal leaders thereof are to be punished by imprisonment for life ;

" 15. Whereas the facts declared to have been proved in the second, third, fourth and fifth " whereases," conclusively show that Don Julio Sanguily y Garit was guilty, through direct participation of the crime defined in the thirteenth " whereas," and has rendered himself liable to the penalty provided for in the fourteenth, because not only was he one of the promoters of the rebellion but was also one of its leaders or principal chiefs, as has been shown to the satisfaction of the court, not only by the data in possession of the court and by the evidence taken at the public trial, but also by an examination and comparison of the documents connected with the third and sixth " whereases," in the undoubted handwriting of the prisoner (which examination the Court performed in fulfillment of the duty made obligatory upon it by Article 726 of the law on criminal trials), and, moreover, by the context of the letter addressed to Betancourt fifteen days before the uprising took place, and by the context of the document taken from Azcuy, inasmuch as appointments of that importance can be made only by the directors or principal leaders of the rebellion ; .

" 16. Whereas, the fact that Don Julio Sanguily was arrested on the morning of the very day on which the uprising took place does not authorize the court to consider him as guilty merely of a frustrated crime or of only an attempt to commit rebellion, because from the letter and spirit of Article 338 it is to be inferred that promoters of the rebellion are liable to suffer the whole penalty even if they are not at the head of any rebel bands or actually sustaining the rebellion, it being sufficient that they have promoted it, and because, it has been satisfactorily shown that Don Julio Sanguily was one of the principal leaders of the rebellion. .

" 17. Whereas, leaving out of consideration the fact that the alternative request of the prisoner's counsel should have been made as an article of ' previo pronunciamiento,' in which case alone it could have been insisted upon at the public trial, according to Articles 666 and 678 of the law governing criminal trials, it is certain that the granting of the requested pardon does not come within the competency of this court, and that on the hypothesis that the prisoner (although he was arrested three days before the publication of the Captain-General's proclamation) was entitled to it, the granting of that pardon is wholly foreign to the jurisdiction of this court, which in the meantime has only to consider the crime punished by the Code, and that there are no subsequent legal circumstances that prevent its punishment, as was declared by the Supreme Court in its decision of July 16, 1873.

"18. Whereas neither the Government attorney nor the counsel for the defense have pointed out any extenuating circumstances, nor can any be inferred from the facts declared to have been proved, and therefore it is proper to impose the mildest penalty provided for the crime, viz., imprisonment for life;

"19. Whereas there is no reason to enforce civil responsibility, and as the costs are understood to be at the charge of those who are guilty of any crime:

"Now, therefore, in view of the articles of the penal code which have already been quoted, and also of articles 1, 11, 12, 26, 53, 62, 79, 89, and 741 of the law governing criminal trials, we pronounce sentence to the effect that it is our duty to condemn, and we do hereby condemn, Don Julio Sanguily to imprisonment for life at hard labor, and to deprivation of his civil rights and subjection to the vigilance of the authorities during his lifetime; and in case the principal penalty be remitted, we condemn him to absolute deprivation of his civil rights and to subjection to the vigilance of the authorities during his lifetime, unless these penalties shall be remitted in the pardon; and we further condemn him to the payment of one-half of the costs of the preliminary examination, and of all those which have been incurred in this case since the public trial was begun; and in view of the investigation made about Sanguily's property, we declare Don Julio Sanguily to be insolvent for the purposes of this case. Thus by this, our sentence, we do pronounce, order, and sign.

"José Pulido,
"Francisco Pampillón,
"Vicente Pardo Bonanza,
"Adolfo Astudillo de Guzmán,
"Rafael Maydagán."

## VII.

### THE APPEAL TO THE SUPREME COURT OF SPAIN.

The record shows that the distinguished lawyer who had
had in his charge the defense of Julio Sanguily, during the
trial ended by the sentence whose full text has been given in
the foregoing chapter, acting with great prudence and looking
above all, as it was his duty, to the good of his client, decided,
as soon as the said sentence was made known to him, to
abandon, at least practically and temporarily, all troublesome
contentions about the treaty rights of the prisoner and the
validity of the proceedings according to which the case had
been conducted, and to use such remedies as the system of
procedure, whether legal or illegal, which had been followed
permitted against the sentence.   Under the Law for the application in the Island of Cuba of the Penal Code of Spain, enacted, as stated before, on May 23d, 1879, the case could be
taken by means of a writ of error to the Supreme Court of
Spain, and Sanguily's learned counsel, seeing that through
this remedy a new chance for his client to obtain justice was
open, and further opportunities were also furnished the United
States Government to get such an accurate and complete information about the facts as was necessary for it to avoid mistakes
and shape its action finally—determined right away to make
use of the remedy which was within his reach, and have the
case submitted to the highest civil jurisdiction in the Spanish
realm.

This determination of Sanguily's lawyer was made known,
among other things, to the State Department by the despatch
of Consul-General Williams to Assistant Secretary of State Mr.
Uhl, of December 7th, 1895. (Doc. No. 104, Senate, 54th
Congress, 2d session, page 42).

Had the learned counsel insisted on the idea, no matter how
well founded, and already presented to the consideration of the
Spanish Government ever since April 25th, 1895, and of the

Court itself (November 12th, 1895), by the solemn protest of Consul-General Williams, in the name of his government (Doc. No. 104, *ibid*, pages 12 and 71), that Julio Sanguily ought to have been tried by such a civil court and according to such proceedings as are provided by the Spanish Law of April 17th, 1821, spoken of in the Cushing Calderón y Collantes Protocol of 1877,—and not by the civil court and according to such proceedings as were competent and legal under the Spanish Law of May 23d, 1879, and other laws subsequent to the said Protocol,—he would have had to acknowledge, under the said law of 1821, that the sentence was final, and would have left his client with no other hope of relief than the interposition in his favor by the Government of the United States of America, whether in the form of a demand, peremptorily made and enforced by ships of war, according to the methods which the Honorable William P. Frye, Senator from Maine, would have resorted to, as he said, if he had had his way, or in some other form, more moderate, and not so much at variance with the habits of diplomacy and civilization.

The risk was run in either case, that before the men-of-war sent to Havana to rescue Sanguily could have reached that port, and succeeded in intimidating the Spanish authorities of the Island of Cuba to the extreme of causing them to surrender the prisoner,—or before any proper diplomatic representations could have reached the Madrid Foreign Office,—Julio Sanguily might probably have found himself crossing the Atlantic Ocean, on board a Spanish vessel, poorly treated, and heavily ironed, on his way to Ceuta, if not already there living the life of a convict.

The wise determination of Sanguily's learned counsel did not prevent the Government of the United States from carrying out its purpose to ascertain, upon real practical knowledge of the facts, whether the treaty rights of Sanguily had or had not been violated. Assistant Secretary of State, Mr. Uhl, wrote to Consul-General Williams, on December 23rd, 1895, as follows " From your dispatch No. 2677 of the 7th instant, and from a letter filed under date of the 13th instant, from Mr. Julio Sanguily, the Department has learned the result of the trial of Mr. Sanguily in the criminal court of Cuba. From these reports of the trial there is reason to apprehend that the proceedings which terminated in Mr. Sanguily's conviction were not in accordance with the treaty of 1795 as construed by the protocol of 1877. It is inferred from the reports that the civil court took up the case against Sanguily where the military tribunal left off, and that the trial proceeded upon the charges formulated and the evidence taken by the military court. It is necessary before taking any action, that the Department should be accurately and fully advised as to the manner in which the trial has been conducted with reference to the Code of criminal procedure and to the provisions of the treaty and protocol. The position of this Government is outlined in a telegram to your office, dated May 21, last (*), to which you are referred. You are instructed to make this report with as little delay as possible, setting forth each step in the proceedings from the first arrest by the military author- ities to the conviction in the civil court." (Doc. No. 104, Senate, 54th Congress, 2nd session, page 70.)

Previously to this dispatch, Mr. Uhl had urged the United

---

(*) *Mr. Uhl to Mr. Springer.* Telegram. Department of State, Washington, May 21, 1895.—Carrillo's case, involving most important principle, has been presented by United States Minister to Spain. In cases Aguirre and Sanguily you will file formal protest declining to recognize validity of military jurisdiction in preliminary stage. The treaty of 1795 excludes the exercise of military jurisdiction altogether, and requires arrests to be made and offences proceeded against by ordinary jurisdiction only. Protocol merely recognizes, declares and explains this treaty right. Military arm has no judicial cognizance over our citizens at any stage. Even arrests, when made by military power, are by a conven- tional figment deemed to have been a civil act. By no fiction can pro- ceedings of military Judge instructor be deemed to be the act of an ordi- nary court of first instance.—Doc. No. 104, Senate, 54th Congress, 2nd session, page 17.

States Consul-General to get a copy of the record of the trial and forward it to the State Department.

But this important instruction could not be complied with, either by Mr. Williams or by General Lee, in spite of their zeal and diligence, because of certain technical difficulties which presented themselves and which neither of those officials could overcome, and more than all, because the counsel for the prisoner, acting with proper haste, had already taken the case, by means of a writ of error, to the Supreme Court of Spain, and as usual in such cases, under the law, the original record had been forwarded to Madrid.

About eleven months after that date, namely, on the 29th of September, 1896, the said Supreme Court reversed the sentence and practically ordered a new trial. The court below was directed to admit in evidence the Betancourt's affidavit which had been rejected in the former trial and to give to it such weight as might be legal and proper.

The following is the text translated into English of the decision of the Supreme Court of Spain:

" In the City and Court of Madrid, on the 29th of September, 1896, in the case taken before us on a writ of error by Julio Sanguily y Garit, appealing from the sentence of the Audiencia of Havana in the proceedings instituted in the first instance against the said Sanguily in the Court of El Cerro District, at Havana, for the crime of rebellion:

"It appearing that the Audiencia of Havana when taking cognizance of this case in the second instance, and subsequent to that stage of the proceedings in which the facts are recapitulated, decided to admit all the evidence offered by both the prosecution and the defense in their respective petitions, and set apart the 28th of November ultimo for the trial:

"It appearing that on the 14th of the same month of November the counsel for the defendant filed an affidavit said to have been just received by mail from the United States, sworn to by Don Pedro E. Betancourt before a Notary Public, stating that deponent had been informed that a letter, supposed to have been addressed to him and signed by one Gener, had been put in evidence against the prisoner, and that the said letter had never been received by deponent, nor has it been seen by him,

nor was he in any manner acquainted with its contents; and
that in filing the said affidavit the counsel for the defense
invoked Article 4th of the Protocol of January 12th, 1877, relating to the construction to be placed upon certain provisions of
existing treaties between the United States and Spain, and
claimed that citizens of the United States are entitled to produce
in their defense, at any time, whatever proofs they may deem
favorable, for all of which he asked the said affidavit to be
admitted as evidence, and ordered to be given the proper
weight as such:

" It appearing that the Audiencia founded on the facts,—that
under Article 656 of the Law of Criminal Procedure, the
whole testimony to be used by each party is to be described in
the petitions called de calificación,—that according to Article
728 of the Code, those proofs so suggested or announced at the
proper time, and no others, are to be admitted, except in the
extraordinary cases marked in Articles 729 and 730 of the Code
relating to steps to be taken by order of the Court, or as a
result of the debates at the time of the trial,—that the said provisions, which had to be strictly obeyed and complied with in
this case, prevented the documentary evidence offered by Sanguily's counsel after the judicially specified time from being
admitted at that stage of the proceedings,—and that even in case
the stipulation of the Protocol of 1877 should be given attention, the petition of Sanguily's counsel could not be granted,
because the protocol, while acknowledging the right of citizens
of the United States to present all the proofs favorable to them,
does not authorize them in any manner to produce such proofs
at a time, or in a form or manner different from the time, form,
and manner provided for by the Spanish Law of Criminal
Procedure,—ruled the said affidavit not to be admitted as evidence and to be returned to the defendant's counsel and that
defendant's counsel noted an exception against this ruling:

"It appearing that on the first day of the trial in the Audiencia,
the defense objected to the examination by a certain expert in
caligraphy designated by the prosecution, of certain letters
and documents, on the ground that the said examination had
been irregularly made in the Court below, without the presence
of the defendant or of his counsel; that the expert who was now
called again to examine those papers, and was the same who
had examined them before, was not at liberty to tell the truth
and thereby change his testimony, because his first deposition
had been made upon oath before the Court below; and that
the first examination, being null and void, could not be validated by such process at that time and at that stage of the

case ; and that the Court founded on the ground that the petition of the prosecution had been filed in due time, and had been granted, and also that the examination of the expert was pertinent, ruled out the objection of the defense, for all of which the defense noted a further exception:

"It appearing that when the decision of the Audiencia was rendered, the defense applied for a writ of error on the ground that Articles 911 and 914 of the Law of Criminal Procedure had been violated, first, because of the non-admission of the evidence offered by the defense, which showed the innocence of the prisoner, and which according to the treaty between the United States and Spain, could be introduced at any time; and second, because the examination of the letters and papers, made a second time by an expert whose first examination was illegal, could not be given any value, because of the impossibility for the said expert to contradict or amend his first testimony made upon oath :

"It appearing that the writ of error was granted, and that the case was brought before this Court in the proper order :

"It appearing that on the day of the trial before this Supreme Court, the prosecution, represented by the Attorney-General, joined the defense in requesting that the decision of the Court below should be reversed, though only on the first ground alleged by the defense :

"The case having been duly heard and examined, Associate Justice Señor Don José María Barnuevo being entrusted to draw up the decision :

"Considering that under Section 1, Article 911 of the Law of Criminal Procedure, cases can be taken to this Supreme Court on a writ of error, whenever the admission of some evidence offered in due time and in the proper form by any of the parties, and deemed to be pertinent, has been refused; that all these circumstances concur in the present case, because the document, which the Audiencia refused to admit as evidence, is pertinent, and has intimate relation with another document filed by the prosecution, the force of which it tends to destroy, and because it was offered in due form and at such a time as it was possible for the defense, which can not be deprived, without good and sufficient reason, of the benefit to be derived by it ; and that for this reason, and not because of the existence of any legal provision authorizing the parties to produce evidence at any time, the document in question ought to have been admitted as evidence, without prejudging thereby its value and efficacy :

"Considering that the second ground on which the defense

has based his action before this Court is untenable, because under the Law, while a remedy is given against orders refusing to admit pertinent proofs, none is given, however, against orders granting their admission.

" We do hereby decide, that the remedy sought for by the defense of Don Julio Sanguily is to be granted on the first ground alleged by the said defense, but not on the second ; and that therefore we must and do hereby annul and reverse the sentence rendered by the Audiencia of Havana in the present case, without costs. And let this decision be communicated to the said Audiencia, in order that the case be restored to the condition in which it was when the admission of the document was refused, and properly continued until its termination, according to law. So, by this, our final decision, which will be published in the *Gaceta de Madrid* and in the *Colección Legislativa*, it has been ordered, adjudged and decreed by us, the undersigned.

' " SANTOS DE ISASA.
" MATEO DE ALCOCAR.
" RAFAEL DE SOLIS LIÉBANA.
" VICTORIANO HERNANDEZ.
" SALVADOR VIADA.
" JOSÉ MARIA BARNUEVO.
" JUAN DE D. ROLDÁN."

## VIII.

THE EFFORTS TO SECURE THROUGH EXECUTIVE SPANISH
CLEMENCY THE RELEASE OF SANGUILY.

The writer of these pages did not receive any authority to
represent Julio Sanguily before the State Department or elsewhere until the 11th of November, 1895, when the day for the
trial of the prisoner at the city of Havana had already been
fixed.  Consul-General Williams had reported on the 2nd of
the same month that the court had decided to begin the said
trial on the 28th following ; and therefore it was useless to
undertake anything until hearing from Havana how the case
had ended.

The short time which elapsed between the 11th of November
above mentioned and the day on which the decision of the
Court of Havana was known at Washington, gave, however,
to the writer of these pages all proper opportunity to see the
papers filed, and to become, through correspondence with his
client and otherwise, fully acquainted with the facts.  He
must confess with sincerity, that the result of his study, as
well as his knowledge of the circumstances which had surrounded the case ever since its inception, led him to the conviction that the Spanish authorities of Cuba would never
voluntarily release his client, as long as the Cuban war should
give the slightest sign of existence.  And as at the same time
he never thought, that in spite of this undoubted Spanish determination to keep Sanguily within the walls of Fortress *La
Cabaña*, more for fear of what he might do, if released, than
for any thing else, there was any reasonable possibility of
turning Sanguily's case into a *casus belli*, or of making it the
subject of belligerent demonstrations or displays of force,
because, as declared by Assistant Secretary of State. Mr. Uhl,
in his note to Consul-General Williams of November 9th, 1895,
there was not, after all, up to that time, any tangible evidence
that the charge of sedition against Sanguily was frivolous

and merely vexatious (Doc. No. 104, Senate, 54th Congress, 2nd session, page 39) ;—the idea occurred to him, very naturally, that the interests of his client would be better subserved by securing, if possible, through diplomatic action, the absolute removal of the case from Cuban influences, either by having it transferred to Madrid together with the prisoner released on bail, or by causing it to be finally terminated through the exercise by Spain of executive clemency, whether in the form of a full pardon, or of such a commutation of the sentence as might involve the freedom of the prisoner.

It was clear to his mind that as long as the circumstances of the war in Cuba should continue to exist, the courts of that Island would never do more in favor of his client, than leaving some door open to further appeals to the Supreme Court of Spain, where the wrongs would be righted, only to the effect of commencing the case *de novo* and having it retried,—and that therefore, to the great detriment of Sanguily's interests, the probabilities were that the case would be protracted indefinitely, going forwards and backwards between Havana and Madrid, until the termination, if ever, of the Cuban war.

Founded upon these reasons, and others equally satisfactory to him, the writer of these pages decided upon a plan of defense, to which his client fully agreed, which substantially embraced the following elements :—

1st. To secure for Sanguily as full and efficient legal defense at Madrid before the Supreme Court as could possibly be obtained ; to see there that every point of law, both international and municipal would be properly attended to; and to make an effort, taking advantage of a well known precedent, to obtain from the said high tribunal a mandate for the release of the prisoner on bail, so as to enable him to personally present himself at Madrid, and appear before the court, if his counsel should deem it necessary, or advisable.

2nd and principally: To secure, if possible, through diplomatic effort the release of Sanguily by Royal command, whether by applying to him the benefits of the decrees of amnesty of Governor-General Calleja, dated respectively February 27th and March 4th, 1895, or by the direct exercise in his favor of the Royal pardoning power.

In harboring the conviction which led him to the adoption of this plan, the writer of these pages did not mean to be unjust towards the court which tried Sanguily, to the extreme of imputing to it any deliberate purpose of doing harm to the prisoner. He merely was afraid that the Court should be subservient. He knew very well what the situation of things in Cuba turns to be when circumstances of the character of those which surrounded the Sanguily case present themselves,—and founded upon experience, he entertained serious doubts about the possibility that anything which might mean in any way whatever judicial independence should exist at that time. He remembered the days of 1869, when a man, but only one,— namely, Chief Justice Don Joaquín Calbetón,—dared to raise his voice, (circular of January 27th, 1869,) urging the courts of Cuba to consider that the first duty of any one entrusted with the administration of justice is to have "civic courage" and resist outside pressure from whatever source it might come, —and he could not see now, when the circumstances were just as bad as in 1869, if not worse, another Señor Calbetón making his bold appearance in the Cuban horizon.

Much less was he guilty, when seeking above all the release of Sanguily through Spanish executive clemency, of sharing in any way whatever the slanderous imputations which so-called friends of Cuba and others have industriously heaped upon the administration of President Cleveland and his Secretary of State Mr. Richard Olney. He knew by his own personal experience, covering more than a quarter of a century of daily contact with the State Department, not to say anything of historical teachings, that in the matter of protection to American citizens against injustice and oppression on the part of Spain, and in the fulfillment of this duty, manly as well as efficiently, the administration of Mr. Cleveland, with Secretary of State Mr. Gresham, and Secretary of State Mr. Olney, has a record, which its enemies cannot obscure, and which challenges comparison with that of all the other administrations which preceded it.

Poor student of history is the one who does not know what that protection was from 1869 to 1884, and how powerful Spain was in this country during those fifteen years. American citizens were murdered in Cuba, sometimes for no other crime than wearing a blue necktie :—one of them was executed, even in violation of a Spanish safe conduct given him by the Spanish Minister;—and in spite of all, even in the case of the *Virginius*, which was settled at the niggard rate of $2.500 per life of an American, Spain was always able to get out of her difficulties, as a prominent Spaniard established in New York telegraphed to Havana, in 1873, in the most graceful manner.

The mere fact that an executive commission was allowed to be established, without the approval of the Senate, and without more formalities than an exchange of notes, to adjust all kinds of claims of American citizens arising out of injuries to the persons or property of American citizens in Cuba during the revolution which broke out in that Island in 1868, and that it was permitted further to remain in existence in Washington for over twelve years, from 1871 to 1883, and to close its sessions leaving more than one-half of the 140 cases which had been referred to it unsettled and undecided for alleged want of jurisdiction, or for other reasons still more futile, not to say anything of the astounding errors which said commissioners were allowed to make in point of law, to such extreme as to have deserved afterwards official condemnation, might be sufficient by itself to demonstrate what the situation was during that period. (*)

(*) Out of eight cases of American citizens killed in Cuba, from January, 1869, to February, 1870, namely: Samuel Alexander Cohner, shot in Havana, January 21st, 1869; Juan Francisco Portuondo, shot near

An Executive Document of the Senate of the United States, No. 108, 41st Congress, 2nd session, shows that on July 9th, 1870, the Spanish authorities of Cuba had already seized five American vessels, killed eight American citizens, unduly imprisoned thirty-six more, and seized and confiscated the property of no less than twenty. All of that went headlong into the deadly waters of the famous arbitration of 1871–1883, where with some disreputable exceptions, the whole thing was wrecked (*). And it shows also, and this is more to the point at issue, that even in the opinion of high officials of the United States Government, officially expressed, the status of American citizens in the eyes of Spain at those eventful days was more than miserable. Admiral Hoff, U. S. N., who had been sent to Cuban waters on an errand of investigation, could not refrain from suggesting, upon absolutely correct comparison, that Great Britain's laws of citizenship ought to have some peculiarity as to efficiently protecting British subjects,— peculiarities well known by the Spanish authorities of Cuba, because, in sad contrast with what usually happened to Americans, British subjects were always shown greater consideration

Santiago de Cuba, in February, 1869; George Bodel, shot on May 24th, 1869; Charles C. Polhamus, shot on June 13th, 1869 ; Charles Speakman, shot on June 16th, 1869; Albert Wythe, shot on June 21st, 1869 ; Ernest McCarty, shot on July 17th, 1869 ; and Vincent Dawney, shot on February 2nd, 1870; only one, namely, the case of Juan Francisco Portuondo, was decided favorably. All the others were dismissed or abandoned. The Portuondo family was awarded $60,000; but the award was not made until after seven years of unrelenting struggle.

(*) The vessels seized were :—The *Mary Lowell*, captured at Ragged Island, on March 15th, 1869;—The *Colonel Lloyd Aspinwall*, captured on the high seas, on January 21st, 1870 ;—The sloop *Champion*, seized at Santiago de Cuba, where she entered in distress, on February 20th, 1869 ;—The schooner *Lizzie Major*, seized on the high seas, on April, 1869 ;—The sloop *Fulton*, seized and mobbed at Havana. The case of the *Lloyd Aspinwall* was submitted individually to two arbitrators in New York, and decided in favor of the United States. All others were either lost or abandoned.

when captured or wrecked upon the Cuban coast. (Ex. Doc. No. 108, Senate, 41st Congress, 2nd session, page 165.)

But leaving all comparisons aside, and returning to the plan of action which the writer of these pages adopted, and to the reasons which induced him to adopt it, the confession must be made further, that at the time of its adoption no indication of any idea to assist Sanguily could at all be perceived either in the horizon of Congress (*) or in the legion of impromptu self constituted defenders, who swarmed around Sanguily as soon as they discovered that his case could be used to harrass the administration of Mr. Cleveland, or to provoke, through Congressional agitation, a conflict with Spain.

The writer of these pages saw from the beginning that his client was safe in the hands of the Honorable Secretary of State, Mr. Olney: that the latter and his subordinates in the State Department had done, and done earnestly and successfully, in favor of Sanguily, in spite of the serious difficulties which the perplexing Cuban problem in its general features brought continually into existence, all that could possibly be done under the law and diplomatic usages. He saw also that the life, as well as the comfort of the prisoner, if comfort can ever be found inside a casemate of Fortress *La Cabaña*, or of any other fortress, had been strongly guaranteed. He saw that the grave question, whether the legal proceedings to which Sanguily was subjected during his trial were or were not regular and in keeping with the treaty stipulations between the United States and Spain, had been handled skillfully and given occasion to strong diplomatic representations, which would be continued and insisted upon, whatever the result of the case might be judicially, and that these representations, as long as the war in Cuba would

---

(*) The resolution introduced in the Senate of the United States, by Mr. Call, of Florida, calling for all papers and correspondence in the Sanguily case,—which was the first Congressional movement ever made on the subject,—was introduced on the 5th of December, 1895, three days after the decision of the Court at Havana.

exist, would never in the end be disregarded by Spain. And he saw, in fine, that after all, in determining to pursue such a course of action as has been indicated, he only followed the example which Sanguily's learned lawyer in Havana had given, when he asked the Court to apply to the prisoner the benefits of General Calleja's proclamation of amnesty, a petition which was not granted, chiefly upon the ground of want of jurisdiction, because the matter was, in the opinion of the court, not judicial, but political and executive.

The first letter which the writer of these pages had the honor to address to the Honorable Mr. Richard Olney, Secretary of State, in behalf of Sanguily, was written in the spirit above explained. It substantially conveyed a request for a diplomatic effort towards securing the release of the prisoner, either temporarily on bail (founded on the Spanish precedent of the case of Don Juan Francisco Ramos), during the pendency of the appeal, or finally through some act of clemency, as well as of comity towards the United States, on the part of Spain. When the prisoner was informed of this movement, he was pleased beyond measure. In his letter of July 3rd, 1896, he said to the writer of these pages: "Hope, which I had lost, has revived in my soul through your action. Do all that you can, my dear friend, to secure my freedom through a pardon (*indulto*), or if not possible in that way, try at least to obtain my release on bail.—But I pray you, to prevent, if possible, my being sent to Madrid."

This latter request alludes to an idea, afterwards abandoned, of the writer of these pages, about which he had had the honor to confer verbally with the Honorable Secretary of State, Mr. Richard Olney, of securing, if advisable and possible, from the Supreme Court of Madrid, a change of venue in the case of the prisoner, so as to have the said case finally tried in the capital of the Spanish monarchy far from Havana and from the passions and influences adverse to Sanguily which appeared to exist in Cuba.

That the Honorable Secretary of State kindly complied with
the wishes of the prisoner's counsel, is shown by this letter.

DEPARTMENT OF STATE,
WASHINGTON, July 9th, 1896.
J. I. RODRIGUEZ, ESQUIRE,
Washington, D. C.

Sir:—In reply to your letter of the 3rd instant, I have to say
that our Minister at Madrid has been instructed to see whether
he can bring about the release of Mr. Julio Sanguily by means
of the provisions of General Calleja's amnesty proclamation of
February, 1895.

This suggestion had also been previously made to Mr.
Taylor in connection with the effort to obtain Mr. Sanguily's
release on bail pending his appeal.

I am, sir, your obedient servant,

RICHARD OLNEY.

The following correspondence, which is published especially
for the purpose of showing how much in earnest the writer of
these pages was in trying to secure the freedom of Sanguily
through some manner of pardon, independently of whatever
action the Supreme Court of Spain might deem proper to take,
will also prove that the diplomatic machinery of the United
States was not as unfriendly to the prisoner, or as slow in acting in his favor, as the enemies of Mr. Cleveland's administration, *cum ira et studio* towards it, not for love to Sanguily, or
even for the sake of principle, have attempted to represent.

WASHINGTON, D. C., July 21, 1896.
Honorable HANNIS TAYLOR,

*Envoy Extraordinary and Minister Plenipotentiary*
*of the United States of America, etc., etc., etc., Madrid.*

Dear Sir:—I know well that when a Diplomatic representative is conducting a negotiation, in the name of his Government
and in behalf of one of his fellow citizens, any attempt of the
latter or of his counsel to make suggestions, or communicate

ideas, no matter how respectfully, might perhaps be considered, with reason, as a kind of intrusion, difficult to be forgiven. And I know better than all, because I, as counsel for the claimant in the Mora case can speak on the subject upon personal experience, that when that diplomatic representative is Mr. Hannis Taylor,—backed by such a man as Mr. Richard Olney, —all suggestions, or communication of ideas besides being blamable in general are particularly unnecessary. But as Mr. Olney told me that he had sent to you my letter on behalf of Julio Sanguily, a prisoner for over sixteen months in the Fortress La Cabaña at Havana, with instructions to do your best to secure the application to him of General Calleja's *indulto* of February 25th, 1895, and as something has happened in Havana of official character which might help your efforts in that direction, I venture to address this letter to you, not without accompanying it with a sincere appeal to your kindness and forbearance.

The prisoner himself has sent to me from Havana, in letter received to-day, the inclosed slip of a newspaper containing the circular issued on the 9th instant by General Weyler of Cuba, indicative of a spirit of comparative leniency towards political prisoners. And I have thought of sending it to you, both because of the absence of Mr. Olney, to whom otherwise I would have shown the paper, and because of the assistance which it might give you, if any, in conducting this negotiation. —If the birthday of Her Majesty the Queen Regent brought about as a very appropriate celebration the freedom of prisoners subject to military jurisdiction in Cuba, why would not the same spirit pervade the spheres of civil justice and aid in securing the liberation of Sanguily?

I beg to be allowed to say, as I had the honor to say to Mr. Olney, and he said that it was true, that every day which is added to the sixteen months of imprisonment which my client has already suffered increases his danger immensely. His safety may be said to be dependent now upon the preservation of the present aspect of the political sky. If for any cause whatever, domestic or international, that sky grows darker: who can foretell what may happen to the prisoner? This is one reason more for which it is to be hoped that the success of your efforts may be speedily obtained.

With feelings of sincere distinguished consideration, I am happy to subscribe myself your obedient servant.

J. I. RODRIGUEZ.

This letter was answered as follows :

Legation of the United States,
Madrid,
San Sebastian, August 14th, 1896.

J. I. Rodriguez, Esq.,
Washington, D. C.

Dear Sir:—I have carefully read your letter of the 21st ult. and I am very willing to tell you in reply of the special efforts which I have made in behalf of your client under the directions of the State Department.

Immediately after receiving the last letter from that source I dined with the Minister of State, and in order to make a final appeal to him personally I took the letter with me and made it the subject of a long conversation after dinner. The result was that the Minister promised me to write a personal letter to the Prime Minister invoking his special interest in the matter. A day or two ago he read me the reply of the Prime Minister, written at great length in his own hand, the substance of which was that while he personally desired to comply with my request he said it was impossible to pardon Sanguily while his brother continued to be one of the most dangerous and bloody of the insurrectionary chiefs. He said that such an act upon his part would cause an outburst of indignation which he could not venture to excite. He further said that Sanguily's case would be heard in the *Tribunal Supremo* on the 19th of September, and if at that time the case should be reversed and sent back for a new trial he would try to have an order made to the effect that Sanguily's imprisonment should be made as comfortable as possible. Beyond this nothing can be expected, as I have exhausted both my personal and official influence in the matter.

I remain,
Very truly yours,
Hannis Taylor.

Far from feeling discouraged by this result, the writer of these pages took advantage of the first opportunity which presented itself to him, to submit again this matter, conversationally, to the attention of the Honorable Secretary of State, and request a further effort in favor of the prisoner, by showing to the Spanish Government how unjust it would be on its part, and how much at variance with its friendly feelings towards the United States and towards the prisoner himself, to make the latter suffer for the alleged doings, whatever they might be, of his brother. It was at that conference, when in discussing the possibility to find out some proper way of removing the apprehensions felt by Spain as to Sanguily's conduct towards her, subsequent to his release, the idea that Sanguily could be paroled was naturally suggested and accepted.

Julio Sanguily, although a Cuban by birth, was a citizen of the United States of America, who in becoming such had solemnly declared on oath, before the court which admitted him to citizenship, that " he absolutely and entirely renounced and abjured all allegiance and fidelity," not only to Spain, but "to every foreign Prince, Potentate or Sovereignty;" foreign in this case meaning "foreign to the United States of America," which certainly includes Cuba. He, as such a citizen of the United States of America, had the plain duty to be, while living in Cuba at least, perfectly neutral in the contest between Cuba and Spain. He had said, furthermore, and insisted upon it repeatedly, that he had had nothing to do with the present Cuban revolution and had kept aloof from it, a statement which was corroborated by the deposition of Don Antonio Lopez Coloma, who paid with his life his allegiance to the Cuban cause and said that he did not think, in spite of what he had been told, Sanguily would ever join the insurrection. In pledging his word of honor not to take arms against Spain, if released, Sanguily besides satisfying his obligations as a law abiding citizen of the United States of America, would not by any means violate any duty belonging to him as a Cuban, because one thing is to be a Cuban and a lover of the liberty of Cuba and of her independence from Spain, and to be ready to sacrifice all things for the success of that undertaking, as Sanguily had done during the war of 1868–1878, and another thing is to approve of and join the revolution which broke out in the Island of Cuba on February 24th, 1895. He had expressed repeatedly, in his letters to the writer of these pages, that he wanted to get out through the *indultoes* of Generals

Calleja and Weyler, and place himself therefore in the legal position of the *presentados*, or men who had abandoned the rebellion and surrendered to Spain. Many a military leader, of great merit and renown, even when engaged in actual war, did not hesitate to submit to the necessities of the occasion and seek for liberty on parole. For these and some other reasons, the writer of these pages deemed it to be his duty to call the attention of his client to the conversation aforesaid and to expectation entertained by him that a negotiation with the Spanish Government, on such a base as this, would probably be successful. Sanguily was left, however, in absolute liberty to decide one way or the other, as the impulses of his heart, or his engagements, if any, might cause him to do.

The letter of Sanguily's counsel, wherein this plan was developed to the proper extent, was not written to him directly for fear that it might fall into Spanish hands. It was written to the United States Vice-Consul General at Havana, Mr. Joseph A. Springer, a common friend of the prisoner and of his counsel here, and in it Mr. Springer was requested to go and see Sanguily, at Fortress *La Cabaña*, or in some other proper way communicate with the prisoner, make him acquainted with the plan, and hear and transmit his decision.

The result of this step can be shown by the following letter:—

UNITED STATES CONSULATE GENERAL,
HAVANA, CUBA, October 22nd, 1896.
JOSÉ IGNACIO RODRIGUEZ, ESQ.,
Washington, U. S. A.

My Dear Sir:—Your letter to Mr. Springer, Vice-Consul here, dated October 13th, has been properly referred to me.

You write that if Julio Sanguily will take his liberty on a pledge or parole, that he will not take up arms against the Spanish Government here, during the continuance of the present war, and that he will not aid, directly or indirectly, the insurgents, as they are called here, during the period above referred to, an effort will be made by the proper authorities to have him released from his cell in Fort "Cabañas," where he has been confined now for some 20 months.

I am prepared to state in reply, that Sanguily will sign any pledge or parole, concerning the points I have named, and that he will leave the Island and reside in the United States, during the war now being waged on it.

I hope this can be done, because of the long confinement Sanguily has already experienced (and the re-trial of his case means, probably, further long imprisonment), and because he is suffering from impaired health and old wounds.

The particular parole to be used might be drawn by the Spanish authorities.

Very truly yours,

FITZHUGH LEE,<br>Consul-General.

The fact that Sanguily as late as September 30th, 1896, was still urging Consul-General Lee, " to insist before the Spanish authorities for his release on pardon under the terms of General Calleja's proclamation of amnesty (see General Lee to Mr. Rockhill, Mr. Sanguily to General Lee, and General Lee to Mr. Sanguily, Doc. No. 104, Senate, 54th Congress, 2d Session, pages 87 and 88), will help to explain the facility, it might be said the eagerness, with which the prisoner acquiesced to be paroled. The letter of his counsel had left Washington, if it left at its date, on the 13th of October, 1896, and nine days afterwards the acquiescence of the prisoner had been expressed.

The writer of these pages was so anxious to secure the release of his client, so sure of the earnest and sincere support which anything conducive to obtain his liberty, or that of any other citizen of the United States of America in Sanguily's predicament, would find on the part of the State Department,—and so fully convinced that the real obstacle which prevented Spain from releasing Sanguily was the fear that he would do, when released, as Aguirre and Carrillo had done,—that without waiting for any further evidence of the determination of his client than the letter of General Lee above copied, communicated at once with the Honorable Secretary of State, transmitting to him the original of the said letter and expressing himself as follows:—

WASHINGTON, D. C.,
October 28th, 1896.

HONORABLE RICHARD OLNEY,
Secretary of State, etc., etc., etc.

Sir :—In pursuance of the conversation I had the honor to have with you, I communicated with Mr. Julio Sanguily, in Havana, and expressed my desire that he should give some pledge, satisfactory to Spain, of his determination not to assist, if released from imprisonment, the insurrection in Cuba. I did not write to him directly, but through the Consulate at Havana, for fear that the letter would not reach him, or that its contents would be revealed to any one except American officials. The letter of General Lee, which I have the honor to inclose, received by me, yesterday afternoon, at a late hour, will show you that Mr. Sanguily will, if released, leave the Island and reside in the United States, and that he will sign any particular parole which the Spanish authorities may draw at their own satisfaction.

I hope that you, having this letter in your possession, will be able to negotiate successfully with the Spanish Government for the release of a citizen of the United States who has been kept in prison ever since February 24th, 1895, who was convicted and sentenced in violation of the law and through errors in the proceedings, which if I am not misinformed have now been ordered to be corrected by a recent mandate of the Supreme Court of Spain.

I am, sir, very respectfully your obedient servant,

J. I. RODRIGUEZ.

The negotiation, however, could not be carried to success as promptly as the prisoner's counsel desired. Whether it was because Spain did not feel satisfied with the manifestations of the prisoner through Consul-General Lee, and needed something stronger or more direct from the prisoner himself, or because of other facts and circumstances which it is unnecessary to explain, the fact is that three months elapsed without any practical result having been obtained.

From the correspondence subsequent to Document No. 104, Senate, 54th Congress, 2nd Session, printed in *Foreign Relations of the United States, 1896*, page 844 and the following, it appears that Sanguily in addition to the verbal statements which General Lee had reported on October 22, 1896, signed on January 21, 1897, one copy in English and another copy in Spanish, of the following paper :

I, Julio Sanguily, an American citizen, confined at *La Cabaña* Fortress, Havana, do hereby sacredly affirm to the United States and to Spain, that if I am released by pardon of the latter Government, I will leave and remain away from Cuba, and will not aid directly or indirectly the present insurrection against the Government of Spain; and I hereby promise that should I do so at any time I will not claim the protection of the United States Government.   I certify that this pledge is given of my own free will and without compulsion on the part of any one.

Fortress *La Cabaña*,
    Havana, January 21st, 1897.      JULIO SANGUILY.

Witnesses : ERNESTO LA FOSCA,
              DONNELL ROCKWELL.

Seven days afterwards, for some reason or other, which the record does not explain, Sanguily signed a second pledge as to his intentions in regard to the former one.   General Lee telegraphed to the State Department, January 28th, 1897, as follows :—

Sanguily signed personal pledge to me that he will faithfully observe terms already mailed.   Recommend case be considered on said terms.   (*Foreign Relations of the United States, 1896*, page 845.)

## IX.

### SECOND TRIAL AND SENTENCE.

While the efforts to secure the pardon of the prisoner, as referred to in the preceding chapter, were being made, the second trial took place, and the second sentence was pronounced.

The new trial began on the 21st and terminated on the 23rd of December, 1896, the Government being represented by the Prosecuting Attorney Señor Don Joaquin Vidal y Gomez, and the prisoner by his new lawyer Doctor Don Antonio Meza y Dominguez. An account of the proceedings was transmitted by Vice-Consul Springer to Assistant Secretary of State Mr. Rockhill, on December 24th, 1896 (Doc. No. 104, Senate, 54th Congress, 2nd session, page 92); and from it and from the accounts of the Havana newspapers, the fact can be disclosed that the defense was conducted substantially on the following grounds: (1) The nullity of all proceedings of military origin and the *a fortiori* inadmissibility in evidence against Sanguily of whatever was done by the Judge Advocate prior to the 16th of March, 1896, when the case was transferred from military to civil jurisdiction :—(2) The futility of the so-called evidence produced against the prisoner:—(3) The denial by the prisoner of having been connected in any way whatever with the Cuban insurrection.

The Havana paper called *La Lucha* published, on December 23rd, 1895, an account of the trial, in which the argument of the prosecution was paid the doubtful compliment of being described as passionate to the extreme, *palpitante de pasión;* and in reality it was no other thing than one of those outbursts of rhetorics, which the Spaniards of modern times call eloquence, and which is their present substitute for past learning and statesmanship. In the opinion of the prosecuting attorney, even the candor, called by him *arrogance*, with which Sanguily admitted to have been a General in the Cuban War of Independence of 1868–1878, was evidence of his guilt,—as it

proved, as he said, that Sanguily was capable of committing
the offense for which he was on trial (*Al ver tan arrogante al
Señor Sanguily lo he creido capaz de su delito*). The past
connection of the prisoner with a war ended seventeen years
ago, had to drag him necessarily, the prosecution said, to join
the insurrection (*sus antecedentes lo arrastran forzosamente á
la insurrección*). The naturalization of Sanguily in the
United States of America rendered him subject, the prosecution
maintained, at least to suspicion (*la segunda naturaleza tiene
que ser sospechosa*). The prisoner in reality was not, in the
opinion of the prosecution, an American citizen, but a Spaniard;
and the reason was, among others, because Sanguily was very
handsome and his vernacular Spanish. (*El Señor Sanguily
en actitud, en figura, en gallardía, lleva aunque no quiera, el
sello de su antigua nacionalidad española.*) Sanguily was guilty
because public opinion pointed at him as a leader of prestige.
(*La opinion pública reconoce en Sanguily uno de los cabecillas
de mas prestigio.*) If Sanguily was not convicted, he, the
prosecuting attorney, although compelled to acknowledge to
have been defeated, would proclaim however not to have been
conquered; and the satisfaction of having complied with the
duty that the Spanish society demanded from him against an
enemy of Spain would always go with him and comfort him.
(*Si el Tribunal lo absuelve, me confesaré vencido, mas no domi-
nado; derrotado, pero no vencido : y me quedaré satisfecho de
haber cumplido con mis deberes y con lo que la sociedad española
exige de mí contra los enemigos de la nación.*)
Such a cheap firework trash seems to have had some effect
with the court. The so-called conclusions which the prosecution had made were accepted, and a sentence, adverse to the
prisoner, was passed on the 28th of December, 1896. Sanguily
was convicted of the crime of rebellion and condemned to
imprisonment for life at hard labor.

This is the text of the sentence :—

"In the city of Havana, on the 28th of December, 1896:"

"This cause of the Government, on the one side, and Don Julio Sanguily y Garitt, a native and a resident of this city, but a citizen of the United States of America, 45 years old, married, engaged in commercial business, the son of Don Julio Sanguily and Doña María Garitt de Sanguily, and a man of learning, having no criminal record, on the other side,—initiated and prosecuted against the latter by the Judge of El Cerro District, for the crime of rebellion,—having been heard and examined by this Section No. 1 of the Criminal Court, all the requirements of law having been fulfilled, the Government having been represented by the Prosecuting Attorney, and Don Julio Sanguily y Garitt by Don Luis Plutarco Valdés as solicitor, and Don Antonio Meza y Dominguez as counsel:

Associate Justice Don Ricardo Maya having been placed in special charge of the case and entrusted with the duty of writing this decision:—

"1. Whereas, the fact appears proved that on the 24th of February, 1895, by order of the Governor General, Don Julio Sanguily y Garitt was arrested at his house in El Cerro District of this city, because the Governor General had received from abroad and from this city confidential information to the effect that Sanguily was one of the promoters of the separatist rebellion which broke out in this Island on that very same day, and that he and Don José Maria Aguirre had been chosen to be the leaders of the revolutionary movement in the provinces of Havana, Matanzas and Santa Clara;—and, furthermore, because according to the reports of the police, which had closely and efficiently watched the movements of Sanguily, the latter had been in communication and correspondence with the Revolutionary Junta of New York and with other foreign abettors of the insurrection, and with the separatist committees secretly organized in this Island; and, finally, because in a report of the Governor of the Region of Havana it was stated that Don Julio Sanguily, owing to his record in the last war, and to the fact that public rumor pointed at him as called to command one of the insurgent bands, had become an object of suspicion, and had been watched by the authorities:

"2. Whereas, the Chief of the Police and Police Inspector Trujillo, when examined before this Court, said that they had not received any express order to watch Don Julio Sanguily, that they knew his separatist ideas because they were publicly known, and that they had no knowledge that he was conspiring when by order of the Superior authority of the Island he was arrested:

"3. Whereas, the prisoner, when examined on the very same day of his arrest, stated that he could not remember to have spoken at all with any person about separatist movements or plans, or received propositions to lead or take part in any uprising : that owing to his political record, he was sure that any serious plan which might have been formed in that line would have been communicated to him ; and that his being entirely ignorant of any such plans was fully proved by the fact that he had not moved from Havana, or even from his house, when he was arrested :

"4. Whereas, the fact is proved that Don Antonio Lopez Coloma, when made a prisoner by forces of the Army at the *Casualidad* Colony, while commanding a body of insurgents which had occupied that place since the 24th of February, 1895, was searched by his captors, and that a letter now forming page 36 of the record, was found in his pocket and reads as follows :—' Cerro, Saturday, the 9th of February, 1895.— Señor Betancourt, Matanzas.—Dear friend : I had intended to have a long talk with you ; but as you are always in a hurry I could not do it. I asked yesterday, Joaquín Pedroso to lend me 25 *centenes* (*) which I needed to go to-day to the country, redeem my revolver and my machete which are pawned, and leave something in my house ; but he did not give them to me. He said that he had not that money. So it is that I cannot move, nor can I even get anything to eat. I wish you would hasten, and this is the purpose of this letter, to get for me just $2,500, not one cent less, which I need. Believe that the situation in my house, if I do not get that money soon, will be difficult. On the other hand, as long as I remain in this situation, my head will not be able to occupy itself of what it is important. Therefore I entreat you to send me the said amount as soon as possible, thereby enabling me to think only of our affair. I cannot find any one here from whom I might borrow 30 or 40 centenes. Had I found such a person I would have gone right away to the country and assisted you in raising the money aforesaid. I have told John to-day that Cervantes had no supper to eat on the day on which he finished *Don Quijote*, and that I, on the eve of placing myself at the head of a work of redemption, find myself so penniless as to have been unable to give my cook any money to go to-day to the market.—Very truly yours,—*Gener*.'

"5. Whereas, the fact is proved that two days before the uprising of the band of Lopez Coloma, the latter came to

---

* A *centén* is a Spanish $5 gold coin.

Havana, by order of Doctor Don Pedro Betancourt, of Matanzas, to see Don Julio Sanguily, Don José María Aguirre, Don
Juan Gualberto Gomez and other individuals, numbering 16
in all, inform them that on the morning of the said 24th of
February, 1895, quite a number of people from Havana would
go to the *Casualidad* estate, where sufficient arms and ammu-
nitions had been deposited, and ask them to place themselves
under the command of said Betancourt, and temporarily, during
his absence, either of Lopez Coloma himself or of Juan Gualberto
Gomez:—and that the letter above copied, signed *Gener*, had
been sent to Lopez Coloma by Betancourt, who, as it seems,
became indignant at the action of the man who wrote it, to the
extreme of doubting his good faith, because, as it appeared, no
part would be taken by him in the movement if the money
asked for was not sent:

"6. Whereas, Don Antonio Lopez Coloma said that he had
not had any conference with Sanguily, whom he only knew
by sight, and that through Betancourt only he knew that
Sanguily and Aguirre should lead the movement:

"7. Whereas, Don Julio Sanguily while constantly denying,
in all the stages of the case, to have had any intervention in
the separatist conspiracy, or to have entered into any engagement with the conspirators, has contradicted the statements of
Lopez Coloma, by saying that the latter came to see him and
tried to induce him to join the rebellion, which he refused to
do, and that he (Sanguily) had endeavored to dissuade Lopez
Coloma, and to show him that the movement was ill advised
and imprudent,—all of which he supplemented by saying that
he had not had with Betancourt any other relations than those
purely social:

"8. Whereas, the fact is proved that the Judge who conducted the proceedings received an anonymous communication
enclosing a letter, which was put on file, for what it might be
worth (page 45 of the record), and reads as follows:—'Cerro,
Thursday, the 14th of February, 1895—Esteemed Friend: I
have been indoors for several days, on account of illness, both
of mine and of my wife.—The latter is still in delicate condition.  Do me the favor to explain this to His Excellency.
I had promised to go and personally confer with His Excellency
about the banished man, Michelena ; but I have been unable
to go out.  I have to communicate something of interest about
this matter, as the police officer is again troubling him.  I
cannot go out and see you to-day, as requested, because I have
taken a medicine ; but I will go to-morrow.  Believe that no
man rejoices more than I that you feel better.—Your affectionate friend.—*Julio Sanguily.*'

" 9. Whereas, it appears that the two letters referred to in the preceding clauses were shown to the prisoner for the purpose of identification ; and that he, in all the stages of the case, persistently denied to have written the one signed 'Gener,' while in regard to the other letter of page 45 of the record, he at first said, during the preliminary proceedings, that the letter was his, and then, during the trial, he doubted the accuracy of his former statement, because the letter which he had really written had been written to a gentleman :

" 10. Whereas, the fact is proved that the experts in caligraphy who examined both letters and compared them with others which are undoubtedly in the handwriting of Don Julio Sanguily, stated their opinion, that, owing to the similarity of the handwriting in all of them, they all were written by the same person,—this identity being in the judgment of the court, upon their own inspection of the documents, a perfectly well-established fact :

" 11. Whereas, the fact is proved that on or about November, 1894, Don Julio Sanguily pawned at the pawnbroker's office called 'La Equitativa,' corner of Compostela and Luz streets. in this city, a machete and a revolver,—and that both articles were sold by the pawnbroker, in April, 1895, with the consent of the prisoner, who was then at *La Cabaña* and expected to be sent to Spain :

" 12. Whereas, the fact is proved that the police of this city having been informed that Don José Inocencio Azcuy was expected to arrive in Havana, on board the American steamer from Tampa, which was due on the 29th of May, 1895, and that he was the bearer of important papers of revolutionary character, waited for his arrival, and arrested him ; and that then, it was found that the said Azcuy carried inside the knot or beau of his necktie a paper which Police Inspector Trujillo seized, but which was snatched from his hands by Mr. Azcuy. who put it in his mouth and endeavored to swallow it, a struggle between the Police Inspector and his prisoner having then taken place, with the result that the fragments in page 236 of the record were recovered :

" 13. Whereas, the fact is proved that shortly before the outbreak of the present separatist revolution Don Nemesio Azcuy sent Don José Inocencio Azcuy to Tampa to bring back to Havana a son of his who was at that place; and that the said Don José Inocencio Azcuy did not succeed in bringing back the young man and returned to Havana without him : that he, while in Tampa, used to call himself a colonel and liked to be addressed in such way, and that Don Enrique

Collazo told him that only in the war the position and the rank of a colonel could be won:

"14. Whereas, the fact is proved both by the testimony of Don José Inocencio Azcuy and by the context of the fragments of page 236, that the paper found in Azcuy's necktie was his commission as colonel in the insurgent army, issued by one who called himself competently authorized to make the appointment, giving him power to organize forces and situate them at the places which he might deem advisable, and to make in his turn such other appointments as were necessary,—all of it written in the handwriting of Julio Sanguily and signed by him, as testified by the experts in caligraphy, whose opinion the court indorses, upon actual inspection and comparison of the handwriting of that paper with all others on file:

"15. Whereas, the fact is proved that two officers of the Civil Guard and the Police Inspector of the town of Aguacate, who had gone in the early part of May, 1895, to the San Rafael estate, belonging to the Portela family, to see some furniture which was for sale there, having obtained permission of a negro woman called Caridad Manzano, who was in charge of the estate, to go through the different rooms of the dwelling house, found in the parlor, hanging on the wall, one carbine which Sanguily has acknowledged to belong to him, and which he says to have used for hunting purposes, whenever he came to that estate, as he frequently did : and that the same officers and Police Inspector found also in a wardrobe several papers, among them a diary kept by Sanguily which has not been offered in evidence, a pamphlet on the independence of Cuba and the letter on file from page 94 to page 97 of the record :

"16. Whereas, the fact is proved that the said letter, written abroad and dated December 9th. 1893, refers to preparations for a rebellion in Cuba, and says that the movement ought to be started in the Island and not outside of its territory,—that he (the man to whom it is addressed) ought not to place himself in a subordinate position, or receive orders from other chiefs, because none was more entitled than him, for his respectability, the guarantee which his name as a revolutionist and a soldier offered the rebellion, and the position that he always had held in the party, to exercise the command,—neither a Sartorius, nor a John Nobody, ought to be allowed in preference to him to claim the glory of having caused the dreams of a part of the population of Cuba to be materialized ;—that he, being a man adored by the Cubans, ought not to allow any other person to occupy his place of honor,— that he ought to start at once and gather the resources necessary for the movement, whether voluntarily, from those who had offered assistance, or by force, he being assured, in the meantime, that proper care would be taken of the support of his family :

"17. Whereas, the fact is proved that this letter, in spite of the opinion of the experts in caligraphy, was not written by Don Julio Sanguily,—because, even if its statements are disregarded, the comparison made by the court between its handwriting and that of the other papers on file, allows the court positively to say that it was written by a different person:

"18. Whereas, the fact is proved that Sanguily registered himself at the office of the Governor-General of the Island, on July 8th, 1889, as a citizen of the United States of America, and that owing to his character as such a citizen of the United States of America the ordinary courts of justice have taken cognizance of this case, under the protocol of 1877 (*):

"19. Whereas, the sentence passed in this cause, on December 2nd, 1895, by Section No. 3 of this Court, was revoked by the Supreme Court, because of the rejection of certain evidence offered on behalf of the prisoner, which evidence, however, has never been produced in the second trial :

"20. Whereas, the prosecuting attorney in submitting his conclusions, stated that the prisoner, Don Julio Sanguily y Garitt, an American citizen since 1878, and a native and a resident of this Island of Cuba, had been, up to the day of his arrest, namely the 24th of February, 1895, one of the most active promoters and instigators of the armed insurrection which broke out on that date against the mother country, for the purpose of securing the independence of this Island; that he had been selected to lead the insurrectionary movement in this province and in those of Matanzas and Santa Clara ; that he, in his capacity of chief and principal leader of the movement and as delegate of the Revolutionary Junta established at New York, had made such appointments, as he had deemed conducive to the success of his plans, as for instance the one of Don José Inocencio Azcuy to be a colonel in the insurgent army ; and that, in view of these facts, the prisoner ought to be adjudged guilty of rebellion, as defined by section

(*) This childish attempt of the court to base the treaty rights of an American citizen, not upon the fact that he is such an American citizen, whether matriculated or not, but upon the fact of his matriculation,—an attempt which has been over and over discredited and defeated,— shows perhaps more strongly than anything else the condition of things which prevailed in Havana at the time of the decision.

1, article 237 of the Penal Code, without any extenuating circumstances, and punished as provided by article 238 of the same, with imprisonment for life at hard labor, and with the other penalties provided by article 53 of said Code, and the payment of half of the costs of the trial:

"21. Whereas, the defence maintained that there was no legal ground to convict Don Julio Sanguily, asked for a verdict of acquital, and claimed in favor of the prisoner, even if convicted, the benefit of the amnesty of February 27, 1895:

CONSIDERING:

"1st. That while in the proper disposition of all criminal cases it is always of interest for the court to become acquainted with the history and the personal record of the party on trial, said record and history being safe guides to pass judgment about the capability or aptness of the said party to commit the offense with which it is charged,—such a knowledge is still more necessary in cases for rebellion, as the commission of a crime of this nature presupposes a clear and well known purpose in that direction on the part of the rebel, and a certain degree of firmness and determination on his part to carry out his criminal purposes:

"2d. That the personal record of Don Julio Sanguily shows that for some years he was fighting in Cuba against the sovereignty of Spain. and that when convinced that he could not separate Cuba from Spain he gave up and relinquished his Spanish allegiance, all of which demonstrates his deep and well rooted separatist sentiments, which as long as concealed within his own mind could escape penal sanction, but which when made public by verbal and written arrangements, and by other punishable acts, serves to reveal that Sanguily's old criminal tendencies have not been changed either through time or repentance;—it being therefore proper for the court in order to form an exact idea of the charge and the proof thereof, to take careful notice of all the facts relating to the prisoner's history, without thereby forgetting that the latter is to be adjudged guilty, or be acquitted only upon evidence relating to the specific charge preferred against him :

"3d. That at the time in which the revolution was about to break out, Don Julio Sanguily y Garitt, was considered by the authorities who are entrusted with the duty of preserving public peace and security as a decided separatist, and that the information transmitted to the superior authority of this Island, subsequently corroborated, represented him as one of the boldest promoters and leaders of the insurgent movement, who was for that purpose in relation with the revolutionary agents abroad and with the separatist committees of this Island,—a charge which is not destroyed or weakened by the fact that neither Don José Paglieri nor Don José Trujillo received special orders, in spite of their positions in the police, to watch Sanguily, because it was optional for the superior authority to use the services of those two officials, or to employ others to assist in the investigation:

"4th. That it is not rash to suppose that the letter found in the house at the San Rafael Estate, which Sanguily frequented so much, was really written to him in 1893, and was his property ; this idea being confirmed by the fact that all the other papers which were found together with the said letter, at the same place and at the same time, and which have been returned to Sanguily, belonged to him, not to say anything of the coincidence between the description made in the letter of the man to whom it was addressed, and the record and the circumstances of the prisoner, a coincidence which is so striking as to leave little doubt of their identity ;—all of which indicates that Sanguily had been conspiring long before his arrest :

"5th. That the explanation given by Don Julio Sanguily for doubting the authenticity of the letter spoken of in the 7th Whereas, which authenticity he had acknowledged in the preliminary examination, is not satisfactory ; that the said letter is therefore to be considered as written by Sanguily; and that this being the case, the other letter referred to in the 4th Whereas, which Don Pedro Betancourt sent to Don Antonio Lopez Coloma, is also Sanguily's, because not only of the absolute identity of the handwriting in both letters, but also on account of other minor details, as for instance the habit of naming the day of the week when writing the date, and the fact that it refers to the pawning of a machete and a revolver, an act which coincides with another of the same nature done by the prisoner :

"6th. That in the said letter Sanguily acknowledged his character of chief of the separatist movement, by lamenting to be so poor when about to place himself at the head of a work of redemption ; a phrase which cannot possibly be misconstrued, either because of its own plain import or because of the feeling of indignation which Don Pedro Betancourt experienced when he saw that a sum of money was demanded by the writer as a condition previous to his lending, as expected, his personal and principal assistance to the insurrection :

"7th. That a further proof of the guilt of Sanguily is the appointment made by him of Don José Inocencio Azcuy to be a colonel in the insurgent army, a fact which shows not only that he took an active part in the preparation of this criminal struggle, but also that he was a chief, because only those who exercise authority can make appointments, or organize the forces which they propose to lead :

"8th. That according to Section 1 of Article 237 of the Penal Code those who publicly rise up in open hostility to the government to proclaim the independence of the islands of Cuba or Puerto Rico, are guilty of rebellion,—and that according to Article 238 of the same Code, those who promote the rebellion, or plan or support it, and are principal leaders, incur the full penalty of the law, even if they do not go to the field and show themselves there in personal and open rebellion against the government,—their character of promoters or leaders being sufficient to render them liable to the punishment provided for in Article 238 aforesaid :

"9th. That Don Julio Sanguily having been recognized as chief by Don Pedro Betancourt in the letter of February 9th, having been waited for by Don Antonio Lopez Coloma to conduct the separatist war in the provinces of Matanzas and Havana, having made appointments of such importance as that which he made of colonel in favor of Don José Inocencio Azcuy, is and must be adjudged, for penal purposes, a principal leader in the insurrection ; and that he is therefore to be punished, with either imprisonment for life at hard labor, or with death, the former penalty to be chosen because of the fact that no aggravating circumstances appear from the record :

"10th. That the weapon belonging to the prisoner, seized at the estate above named, must be confiscated, as provided by article 71 of the Code: and that the prisoner must also be condemned to pay the costs of the trial:

"11th. That the benefits of the amnesty of February 27th, 1895, are not applicable to Don Julio Sanguily who did not surrender himself to the proper authorities:

"Upon examination of the articles above cited of the Penal Code, and of articles 1, 11, 12, 26. 53, 62, 78 and 89 of the same. and article 741 of the Law of Criminal Procedure ;

"We do hereby decide: that we must condemn, as we do, Don Julio Sanguily y Garitt to imprisonment for life at hard labor, with the accessory penalties of deprivation of civil rights and perpetual vigilance by the authorities,—and in case that he be granted a pardon, and thereby be relieved from the imprisonment, to perpetual disability and subjection to perpetual vigilance by the authorities, unless these two penalties are also expressly wiped out in the pardon,—and to the payment of one half of the costs of the trial. We declare furthermore that the weapon seized in this case must be forfeited to the use of the Government and that it should be delivered to the Military Governor of this city : and finally, and for the purposes of this sentence, we do also declare the prisoner to be insolvent.

" And by this our sentence, we have so adjudged, ordered and decreed. Witness our hands.

" RICARDO MAYA,

" JUAN VALDÉS PAGÉS,

" ADOLFO ASTUDILLO DE GUZMÁN,

" MANUEL VÍAS OCHOTECO,

" JOSÉ NOVO Y GARCÍA."

## X.

### THE COMMUTATION OF THE SENTENCE AND THE RELEASE OF THE PRISONER.

How little practical effect can be put to the credit of the foregoing decision, in spite of its length and its elaborate pomposity, can be easily discovered by a simple comparison between its date, and the date of the release of the prisoner. The sentence had been passed on the 28th of December, 1896,— and less than two months afterwards, on the 25th of February, 1897, the man whom it condemned to imprisonment for life in chains and at hard labor, had recovered his liberty, gone out of the fortress where he had been kept for two years, and allowed to return, as he had promised, to his adopted country.

Sanguily's lawyer in Cuba had taken an appeal, as it was his duty, against the sentence of the Court, and had fixed every thing in the proper shape so as to insure that the case should again be transferred, upon a writ of error, to the Supreme Court at Madrid. But this prudent step, which no other man of the professional eminence which Sanguily's counsel had deservedly reached would have failed to take, gave, however, occasion to a somewhat serious difficulty, which thanks to his good sense could be promptly removed.

The interposition of the appeal, which paralyzed for a moment the diplomatic effort, had practically the effect of obstructing, *pro forma* at least, the realization of the agreement which had been entered into between the two governments, because it was alleged, and alleged with reason, that the pardoning power of Her Majesty the Queen Regent of Spain could not, under the laws, be called into exercise, until after the sentence of the court had become final(*). And it was

(*) Even Senator Frye, who was so unmerciful in scolding Sanguily's lawyer for the withdrawal of the appeal, had to admit that otherwise the release of Sanguily could not have been then obtained Spain, he said, "could not pardon him (Sanguily) until he was a sentenced criminal, which is the law of all nations."—(*Congressional Record*, 54th Congress, 2nd Session, February 25, 1897, page 2383.)

for this reason that the Spanish Government, while reaching the conclusion to comply with the wishes of the United States, by releasing Sanguily from imprisonment, as it was duly communicated to the State Department, suggested also, separately, that in order to expedite matters the appeal which had been taken should be withdrawn.

This suggestion was made in the following manner:

LEGATION OF SPAIN IN WASHINGTON,
February 22nd, 1897.
(Personal and private.)

Mr. Secretary:—Referring to the confidential note which I have had the honor to address to Your Excellency, on this date, relating to the American citizen Julio Sanguily, I have the honor to inform Your Excellency confidentially that in order that the benevolent intentions of H. M. the Queen Regent of Spain with regard to that citizen may take effect, it is necessary that he should withdraw the appeal which he has taken against the sentence of the court which condemned him.

It is absolutely necessary under the Spanish laws that in order that Her Majesty may exercise the right of pardon the sentence should be final.

The Minister of the Colonies in obedience to the order of the Council of Ministers has telegraphed to Cuba to have the necessary proceedings expedited, in case that Sanguily, or his counsel, withdraws the appeal taken.

When this is done, and when the pardon can be decreed in accordance with the law, it will be communicated by cable.

I avail myself, Mr. Secretary, etc., etc.

E. DUPUY DE LOME.

HON. RICHARD OLNEY,
etc., etc., etc. (*)

Upon the receipt of this letter the Honorable Secretary of State telegraphed to Consul-General Lee at Havana, in the following language:

(*) A copy of this letter was given by the Honorable Secretary of State, Mr. Richard Olney, to the Honorable Chairman of the Committee on Foreign Relations of the United States Senate, on the 24th of February, 1897. It was published in full with other papers in the Washington *Post* of February 28th, 1897.

DEPARTMENT OF STATE,
WASHINGTON, February 23d, 1897.

Inform Julio Sanguily and his counsel that in order to perfect issuance of pardon, appeal should be withdrawn and notice of withdrawal at once given here and in Madrid.

OLNEY.

The response which was given to this dispatch was prompt and satisfactory. No hesitation was shown. No questions were asked. No doubts were entertained. Full reliance was placed upon the action of the distinguished head of the Washington State Department, and all the papers necessary to effectually withdraw the appeal were prepared on the same day and properly filed.

Consul-General Lee reported this fact on the 24th of February, 1897, by the following telegram:—

Have absolute withdrawal of appeal Sanguily's case. Can so cable Madrid. It is understood, of course, if not pardoned, appeal be again taken, as withdrawal leaves original sentence in full force.

By the removal of this impediment the consummation of the plan practically agreed upon since early in February(*), could be effected at once. Her Majesty the Queen Regent could then, with no impropriety, exercise her high prerogative. And so she was pleased to do by the following decree :

In conformity with the opinion of my Council of Ministers, and in use of the power vested in me under section 3rd, article 24, of the Constitution :
Upon inspection of the law of June 18th, 1870, which

---

(*) A letter of the Honorable Secretary of State, Mr. Richard Olney, to the Honorable Chairman of the Committee on Foreign Relations of the United States Senate, Mr. John Sherman, dated February 17, 1897, and published in the Washington *Post* of February 28, 1897, states that "a cable from Madrid ordering the release (of Sanguily) may be expected any moment."

regulates the exercise of the pardoning power, and acting in accordance with articles 3rd, 21st and 29th of the same law :

Considering that the Government of the United States has friendly and confidentially communicated with the Government of Spain, and asked the pardon of Julio Sanguily, an American citizen, condemned by the Audience of Havana, in a cause for rebellion, to imprisonment for life at hard labor,—said application being founded upon the facts that the prisoner has suffered already about two years of incarceration, that while he, the said prisoner, could possibly, at the outbreak of the insurrection in Cuba, have endangered there the safety of Spain, such is not now the case under the very different circumstances which exist at present, and that he, the said prisoner, has solemnly pledged his word to the two Governments, as set forth in writing by him, that he will not aid directly or indirectly the present insurrection :

In the name of my august son the King Don Alfonso XIII., and as Queen Regent of the kingdom :

I do hereby commute into perpetual banishment and the disabilities incident and subsequent thereto the penalties of imprisonment for life at hard labor and civil interdiction imposed upon Don Julio Sanguily by the Audience of Havana in cause for rebellion.

Given at Palace on the twenty-fifth of February, eighteen hundred and ninety-seven.

MARIA CRISTINA.

TOMAS CASTELLANOS Y VILLAROYA,
*Minister for the Colonies.*

As this decision of Her Majesty was transmitted at once by cable to the Governor-General of Cuba, the official who was acting as such, during the absence of General Weyler, could write almost immediately to Consul-General Lee, in the following terms:

HAVANA, February 25th, 1897.

The Minister of the Colonies telegraphs to me to-day that Her Majesty the Queen Regent has signed a decree commuting the penalties of perpetual imprisonment and civil interdiction imposed by the Audience of this territory on the American citizen Mr. Julio Sanguily, into that of perpetual exile and its accessories.

And as I have ordered that the command of Her Majesty be complied with, I have the honor to inform you of the above, as well as of the fact that proper instructions are now being given for the immediate release of the prisoner, so as to enable him to leave this port for the United States by the steamer sailing next Saturday, the 27th instant.

May God preserve you many years.

EL MARQUÉS DE AHUMADA.

A few hours afterwards, Sanguily found himself, a free man again, in the office of the United States Consul-General at Havana, and together with his family and friends commenced his preparations to depart from Cuba.

The writer of these pages, to whom the Honorable Secretary of State had the kindness to inform, almost instantly, that Sanguily had been released,—as Consul-General Lee immediately reported by cable,—was favored on the day following, with the following communication :

WASHINGTON OFFICE OF THE CHICAGO RECORD,
WILLIAM E. CURTIS,
Post Building.

WASHINGTON, D. C., February 26, 1897.

My Dear Doctor :—Mr. Dupuy, the Spanish Minister, has just telephoned that Sanguily will sail from Cuba on the Plant Line to-morrow (Saturday), and that he (Mr. Dupuy) is very anxious that you should know it at once, and not having your address he asks me to inform you.

Very truly yours,

J. T. SUTTER, JR.

This act of courtesy, so much the more to be appreciated as it was purely spontaneous and gracious, completed the information of Sanguily's counsel in this country and caused his mind to be at rest.

Three days afterwards, Julio Sanguily himself telegraphed to him (March 2nd) from the S. T. Depot, Tampa, Florida, announcing his safe arrival.

## XI.

### CONGRESSIONAL INTERFERENCE.

Nine months and eleven days had elapsed since the imprisonment of Julio Sanguily, when the idea first occurred to some alleged friend of the prisoner to start Congressional action in his behalf. Undue advantage was taken undoubtedly of the overflowing generosity which in favor of Cuba was always shown by the Honorable Mr. Wilkinson Call, Senator from Florida, where the voting element is largely Cuban, and where, if organized and disciplined, the said vote would perhaps be decisive, and an effort was made, successfully, to induce him to interfere in the prosecution of the case, without consulting at all with the State Department, or putting himself in touch with the prisoner's regularly constituted agent or representative.

Up to that time the defense of Sanguily had never transgressed the limits of judicial or diplomatic action ; but from this moment forward a new element forced itself in the case, which owing to its independence, to its being prompted principally by political reasons, and to the facilities which it afforded to create irritation, imposed upon the parties to which the interests of the prisoner were legitimately entrusted additional anxieties.

This first interposition consisted in a resolution which some one, not sufficiently familiar with the requirements of form and courtesy prevailing in such cases, had prepared for the Honorable Mr. Call, and which he consented to introduce in the Senate of the United States, on the 5th of December, 1895, reading as follows:

*Resolved,* That the Secretary of State be directed to send to the Senate all the correspondence relating to the trial, conviction and sentence to hard labor for life of General Sanguily, an American citizen, for alleged complicity in the war against Spain by the Cubans; and if no authentic record should be on file in the State Department, that the Secretary of State be directed to obtain a copy of the record of such trial.

The record shows that this resolution having been considered by unanimous consent of the Senate, and agreed to, was communicated to Consul-General Williams, on December 7th, 1895, by Assistant Secretary of State Mr. Uhl, with instruction to ask and forward to the State Department as soon as practicable a certified copy of the record of Sanguily's trial. (Doc. No. 104, Senate, 54th Congress, 2nd Session, page 69.)

The fact that in the opinion of some people something grand had been gained by causing, as upon the face of the resolution could be maintained, the Senate of the United States to ignore the President, to use twice in seven lines imperative language in addressing the Secretary of State, as if the latter official were a subordinate of the Senate, to designate Sanguily by no other name or title than that of General, and to term the Cuban struggle "the war against Spain by the Cubans," fortunately produced the effect of satisfying the authors of the measure and quieting their ardor.

Whether it was for this, or for some other reason, that this movement was allowed to die out, without the slightest effort having been ever made to find out what had become of the "mandate" of the Senate, it is unnecessary to investigate. But the fact is that the Honorable Mr. Call's resolution was followed by a period of fully thirteen months of absolute repose, in which the diplomatic Department of the United States, and the counsel for the prisoner, each one in its proper sphere, were left undisturbed.

But on the 5th of January, 1896, the Honorable Mr. Call got up again in the Senate of the United States and said as follows:

Mr. President: I submit two resolutions, which I ask may be read and printed, and lie over, under the rule, until to-morrow morning, when I shall submit some observations upon them.

One of these resolutions, evidently prepared by him personally, framed in proper language, and aiming at nothing which was not practical and reasonable, was couched as follows:

*Resolved*, That the President be, as he is hereby, requested to send to the Senate, if in his opinion not incompatible with the public interest, all the correspondence and reports of the Consul-General of the United States at Havana, relating to the arrest, imprisonment, trial and condemnation to perpetual imprisonment in chains of Julio Sanguily, a citizen of the United States, by the authorities of Spain in Cuba.

The other, acknowledged by the Honorable Mr. Call to have been "prepared by an eminent citizen in Havana, who is cognizant of all the facts connected with the case, and a man of high character,"—and "to reflect the opinions, the feelings and the judgment of a man whose name, if it were permitted to disclose it, would carry conviction with it everywhere " (Congressional Record, 54th Congress, 2nd Session, page 489), was given by the Senate, with the consent of the Honorable Mr. Call, the form of a joint resolution,—thereby becoming subject to the action of the House of Representatives and to the approval of the President. Its language is the following:

Whereas, Julio Sanguily, an American citizen, arrested in his home in Habana the day before the outbreak of the present insurrection, has been confined in his cell in the Cabañas prison for the past twenty-three months ; and

Whereas, the lawyer who defended him in his first trial has also been imprisoned in said prison ; and

Whereas, his principal witness, Lopez Coloma, was shot in said prison by order of the Spanish authorities immediately preceding the second trial of said Sanguily ; and

Whereas, the attorney who conducted the proceedings in the appeal before the authorities at Madrid has since been deprived of his office and emoluments attached thereto by the authorities at Madrid in consequence thereof ; and

Whereas, the said Julio Sanguily has been tried and condemned to perpetual imprisonment in chains, without evidence against him and without the opportunity of defense: Therefore,

*Resolved, by the Senate and House of Representatives of the United States of America in Congress assembled*, That the President of the United States be instructed to demand the immediate release of the said Julio Sanguily with permission to return to the United States.

The wishes of the Honorable Senator were complied with, and the resolutions were read and allowed to wait, without action, until the day next following.

The record shows that on that day (January 6th, 1896) the Honorable Senator from Florida, after having caused both resolutions to be read again by the Secretary, said: "I ask that the resolution requesting information may now be accepted." To this the Senate agreed, and the resolution was passed. (Congressional Record, 54th Congress, 2nd Session, page 485.)

Immediately afterwards he took up his second resolution demanding the release of Sanguily, which he acknowledged, as has been quoted, not to have been prepared by him but by an eminent citizen, etc., etc., and embarked into a lengthy speech, which covered other cases besides Sanguily's, and dealt most principally with the question of Cuba, the Cuban war, and the necessity for the United States to assist the insurgents in wiping out from Cuba the power of Spain. His purpose was, apparently, to put himself on record, once more, on these matters, without aspiring however, for the moment at least, to any practical result. "I move," he said: "that the joint resolution be referred to the Committee on Foreign Relations and I hope for speedy action on the matter." (Congressional Record, 54th Congress, 2nd Session, page 489.)

In the course of his speech, the Honorable Mr. Call found the way to repudiate a second time the paternity of the joint resolution which he had consented to introduce. He said : "The statements and the preamble of the above resolution were made by persons of character and veracity, and the evidence as submitted to me from such witnesses authorizes me to say that they are true. I am informed from reliable sources that evidence of the facts as above stated is to be found amongst the files of the State Department." (*Ibid* page 486.) Perhaps, on this account, the responsibility which befalls him for stating that "Mr. Sanguily could not secure the services of any lawyer to prosecute his case,"—that the prisoner was kept in solitary confinement, and "not allowed to see, or to have communication by letter, or otherwise, with any person except the authorities immediately in charge of him," and that "a witness who could have proven Sanguily's entire innocence, namely, Lopez Coloma, was a few days before his last trial taken from his cell in the Cabañas, where he had been imprisoned for a considerable time, and shot without any trial, as Sanguily said, for the purpose of preventing him from testifying" (*Ibid* page 486), is not as grave as might have been otherwise.

The Senate, which had listened to these remarks, and to some others elicited by them, decided to comply with the wishes of the Honorable Mr. Call and ordered the joint resolution to be referred to the Committee on Foreign Relations.

The fact must not be forgotten that although the Honorable Senator from Florida declined to explain in the Senate, what the sources of his information were, and said : "I am not at liberty to give the name,"—he came nevertheless, on the following day (Congressional Record, January 7th, 1896, page 545), and asked "unanimous consent to present a paper from a gentleman who has been elected as a Republican member of the next Congress, who has recently been in Havana." He moved, further, the said "statement to be read and printed in the Record,"

As this motion was agreed to, the record of that day's session contains a statement prepared and signed by Mr. Edward E. Robbins, which in the part relating to Julio Sanguily, reads as follows :

I also had a talk with Julio Sanguily, who stated that he had been confined in the Cabañas for a period of twenty-three months. It appears from his statement that the day before the rebellion broke out in Cuba, while taking a bath in his house, he was arrested and thrown into prison. He was tried and condemned to punishment by a military tribunal, the sentence being that he should be punished perpetually in chains, etc. The United States authorities protested, on the

ground that Sanguily was a citizen of the United States, he
having been naturalized in New Orleans and having resided
there for some time, and that he was taken without arms and
should be tried by the civil authorities and not the military
authorities.  An appeal was taken to the authorities at Madrid,
and this sentence was set aside.

He was retried and a few days ago a similar sentence imposed upon him.  The lawyer who conducted the first trial of
Sanguily was also thrown in prison, and is now in the Cabañas
along with Sanguily.  The lawyer who managed the appeal in
Spain has been deprived of his office and all emoluments attached thereto by the authorities at Madrid.  A witness who
could have proven Sanguily's entire innocence, namely, Lopez
Coloma, was a few days before this last trial taken from his
cell in the Cabañas, where he had been imprisoned for a considerable time, and shot without any trial, as Sanguily said, for
the purpose of preventing him from testifying.

An appeal must be taken within a few days, or, unless the
United States interferes, the witness (*sic*) will be transferred to
the penal colony in North Africa, in accordance with the sentence
passed a few days ago.   Sanguily stated that he did not believe
that he could get any lawyer to take his case and conduct his
appeal, as the fate of his other two lawyers who conducted the
former proceedings would deter others from undertaking the
case again.

Sanguily seems to be a man of about sixty years of age, quite
gray, and complained that the imprisonment, during the past
twenty-three months, was breaking his health, so that he could
not longer endure it : and he desired that the United States
Government take action in his case at once, by inquiring into
the cause of his detention and the unfair method by which he
has been tried and convicted.  He claims that there is no possible testimony as to his being implicated in the rebellion, but
that he was simply confined because he might perhaps have
been guilty of some offense in the future, yet that he was guilty
of no offense whatever when arrested, and nothing was proven,
or could be proven against him.

In response to the request of the Senate, President
Cleveland transmitted to that body, on February 1st, 1897, a
report from the Secretary of State, accompanied by copies of
correspondence concerning the Sanguily case; and the papers
so sent were referred by the Senate to the Committee on Foreign
Relations, and ordered to be printed.  They form the matter

of a printed pamphlet of 96 pages, entitled Document No. 104 of the Senate, 54th Congress, 2nd session, on the " Arrest, imprisonment, etc., of Julio Sanguily,"—which was reprinted, first, as an "Appendix" to the Senate Report No. 1534,—and subsequently with several additions, as a part of the volume entitled *Foreign Relations of the United States in 1896*, from page 750 to page 846.

Upon consideration of these papers, the Committee decided to set aside the Joint Resolution introduced by the Honorable Mr. Call, which had been marked "Senate Resolution No. 186," and report as a substitute, another one which was marked "Senate Resolution No. 207" and reads as follows :

*Resolved, by the Senate and House of Representatives in the United States of America in Congress assembled,* That the Government of the United States demands the immediate and unconditional release of Julio Sanguily, a citizen of the United States, from imprisonment and arrest under the charges that are pending and are being prosecuted against him in the military and civil courts of Cuba upon alleged grounds of rebellion and kidnapping, contrary to the treaty rights of each of said Governments and in violation of the laws of nations.

And the President of the United States is requested to communicate this resolution to the Government of Spain, and to demand of that Government such compensation as he shall deem just for the imprisonment and sufferings of Julio Sanguily.

This resolution was submitted in behalf of the committee by the Honorable Mr. John T. Morgan, of Alabama, on the 24th of February, 1897, together with a quite lengthy report (Senate Report No. 1534, 54th Congress, 2nd Session), which was ordered to be printed and placed on the calendar.

In making this submission, the Honorable Mr. Morgan said: " I am directed by the Committee on Foreign Relations to report a joint resolution which I ask may be read at length. The Committee thought it was their duty to request very early action upon the joint resolution, but inasmuch as one or more members of the Committee were absent at the time, who had not the opportunity of understanding the whole subject, it may be better that I should give notice, and I will do so, with the concurrence of the Honorable Chairman of the Committee, * * * that in the morning hour to-morrow the joint resolution will be called up for action."

The Honorable Mr. John Sherman, Senator from Ohio, and Chairman of the Committee on Foreign Relations having expressed his assent to letting the resolution lie over until the following day, an order was made accordingly. (Congressional Record, 54th Congress, 2nd session, pages 2305 and 2306.)

It seems to be the fact that during the twenty-three days which elapsed between the reference to the Senate Committee on Foreign Relations on February 1st, 1897, of the papers relating to this case which the President of the United States had sent to the Senate, together with a report from the Secretary of State, and the day on which the Honorable Mr. Morgan submitted the report of the Committee, the chairman of the latter had interested himself considerably, as it was just, in the consideration of the subject, and made, as proper and usual in such cases, by correspondence and otherwise, such inquiries at the State Department as were necessary to aid him in reaching a right conclusion, and in conducting properly the deliberations of the important body over which he presided.

The Honorable Mr. Richard Olney had said in his report, that "in view of all the circumstances of this case, and especially of the long imprisonment already suffered by the accused, representations have been made to the Spanish Government, which it is believed will not be without effect, that the case seems to be one in which executive clemency may be reasonably exercised," and when, as it appears, the idea came to the mind of the Honorable Mr. John Sherman, Chairman of the Committee, in consequence of that statement, to send a message, seventeen days afterwards to the Honorable Secretary of State, asking him for information about the present condition of the case, the Honorable Mr. Olney responded as follows :

DEPARTMENT OF STATE.

WASHINGTON, February 17th, 1897.

DEAR MR. SHERMAN:

In reply to your message of to-day about the Sanguily case, I desire to say for your own use and information, exclusively, that since my report of February 1st, certain confidential communications have taken place between this Government and the Spanish Government, which I confidently expect to result in Sanguily's release. Indeed, I am given to understand that a cable from Madrid ordering the release may be expected any moment.

The matter is of a somewhat delicate nature, and I shall be very sorry to have the present favorable prospects for Sanguily's release injuriously affected, as they would be very likely to be by any public discussion of the case in the Senate, or elsewhere.

Very truly yours,

RICHARD OLNEY.

HON. JOHN SHERMAN,
*United States Senate.*

Four days after this letter, and three before the date in which the Honorable Mr. Morgan submitted to the Senate the report of the Committee of which he was such a distinguished member, the negotiations, to which the Honorable Secretary of State had alluded in the foregoing communication, were ended successfully, the Spanish Government having agreed to accede to the wishes of the United States, and advise Her Majesty the Queen Regent of Spain to exercise in favor of Julio Sanguily her pardoning power.

Reference has been made in the foregoing chapter to the letters addressed by the Spanish Minister in Washington to the Honorable Secretary of State, on February 22nd, 1897, reporting in one the conclusion reached by the Spanish Government, and suggesting in the other the proper manner of removing the purely technical obstruction which had been encountered in carrying into effect that decision.

The facts have been explained furthermore that telegraphic instructions were sent to Havana on the 23d of February, 1897,

by the Honorable Secretary of State to the United States Consul-General there, concerning the withdrawal of the appeal ;
that the United States Consul-General telegraphed back on the
day following (February 24, 1897) that the appeal had been
withdrawn as desired ; that information of these facts was instantly transmitted by cable to Madrid ; and that the Honorable Secretary of State in pursuance of the policy which he had
adopted of keeping the Honorable Chairman of the Senate Committee on Foreign Relations well posted with all that happened
in the case, provided him with a copy of the note addressed to
him by the Spanish Minister on the 22nd of the same month(*)
and has been printed elsewhere.

Whether the Honorable Mr. Morgan knew, when he submitted his report on the 24th of February, 1897, that the
culmination of this business had been successfully reached
three days before; or whether he, on that memorable 25th of
February, 1897, urged the passage of Senate Resolution No.
207, knowing that the case was settled, and that the decree of
Her Majesty the Queen Regent of Spain, releasing Sanguily
from imprisonment, was being flashed by cable to the city of
Havana, and the gates of *La Cabañas* Fortress being open to
the prisoner, it is unnecessary to investigate. But the fact is
that notwithstanding the utter uselessness of the proposed
measure, it gave occasion to one of the most extraordinary and

(*) Mr. Olney's letter reads as follows:

DEPARTMENT OF STATE,
WASHINGTON, February 24, 1897.

HONORABLE JOHN SHERMAN,
*Chairman Committee on Foreign Relations,*
*United States Senate.*

Sir : Referring to the case of Julio Sanguily, I am just in receipt of a
note from the Spanish Minister at this capital, copy of which (in translation) I herewith inclose.

Respectfully yours,
RICHARD OLNEY.

The inclosure has been printed in page 81.

excited debates which have ever been witnessed in the Federal Senate.

True it is that as shown by the Record (page 2382, Congressional Record, February 25th, 1897), that passionate discussion, where no consideration whatever was shown either to the Government of the United States, the Government of Spain, or historical truth, was not held in the Senate properly, but in the Senate, *as in Committee of the Whole*, a fact which deprived the speeches, as well as the measure itself, of all immediate practical importance, as it rendered it necessary for the resolution, even if passed without amendments, to be reported to the Senate, and be subject again in it to amendments and debate (*). But the freedom of speech, and the absence of parliamentary restraint, which were displayed in this case, although proper and necessary in all Committee discussions, and much more in Committees of the Whole, which were devised precisely to facilitate the free exchange of views, open the valve to passion, and thoroughly shake up the subject, until finding the truth,—created a situation of great danger for the liberty of Julio Sanguily, and even for the maintainance of the good relations between the United States and Spain.

Such a distinguished Senator as the Hon. John W. Daniel, from Virginia, carried away by his sympathy and good will towards the prisoner, was heard to represent the latter as "languishing sick and sore and wounded in the Cabañas Fortress in Havana,"—as "treated rigorously, harshly, cruelly, and brutally,"—as dealt with in a manner which "is a disgrace to this century and to civilization,"—and as "compelled by sickness, by poverty, by delay, and by the failure of his own Government to defend him" * * * "to withdraw the appeal as a condition of his liberty." The Honorable Senator exclaimed: "If I represented this country in any place in which

---

(*) It has been seen very often, even in the discussions affecting the Cuban question, that at the moment of voting, many an ardent supporter of extreme measures has failed to be present.

I could act with authority, I should telegraph Sanguily not to withdraw his appeal.''

When in response to this vehement peroration the Honorable Mr. Eugene Hale, Senator from Maine, read a telegram announcing that Sanguily's lawyer had filed the proper papers withdrawing the appeal, his colleague, the Honorable Mr. William P. Frye, Senator from the same State, did not hesitate a moment in declaring that that distinguished lawyer had ''done an exceedingly wicked and unjust act towards his client'' indulging afterwards in the utterance which brought down upon him the applauses of the galleries, that if he had his way, ''a ship of war would start forthwith to Havana and deliver him.''

Things were carried to such an extreme as to cause the Honorable Mr. W. V. Allen, Senator from Nebraska, to say that it had become necessary to test in some way, '' whether there was really any sincerity '' in all that noise. The Honorable Mr. John M. Palmer, from Illinois, was forced also to remind the Senate that there was in the White House ''a bold, brave, patriotic, manly statesman, whose purpose is to enforce the laws of the country and international law,'' on whom the American people could rely, and to say in addition that he had listened to the debate attentively, and regarded it ''as a mere tempest in a teapot.''

The Honorable Mr. John T. Morgan, from Alabama, who stated, no doubt upon good authority, that Sanguily ''refused absolutely to participate in the present rebellion'' because he had ''some recollections of what he had suffered before,'' because ''his wounds would have kept him out of military service,'' and because ''his age would have prohibited him from going into military service,'' referred to the first examination of the prisoner by the military Judge Advocate as an ''Inquisition process, worthy of the strong condemnation, performed without the presence of counsel, or of witnesses.'' (Congressional Record, February 25, 1897, page 2379.)

In the report of the Committee, which the Record shows was never read in the Senate (*), many statements are found to the same effect as those copied. It repeats the assertion that "a military officer subjected Sanguily to an inquisitorial examination at 11 o'clock at night, without the presence of witnesses or of counsel ; " and states that Sanguily "is now an old and feeble man, still suffering from severe wounds received in battle." But the principle is strongly vindicated by it, that the duty of American citizens to their own country, while residing abroad, involves respect and obedience to the laws of their domicile. "It is only just and in accord with the well established opinions of mankind," the report says referring to Sanguily, "to attribute to a man, who has exhibited high courage and devotion to honorable duties,—of which his many wounds are eloquent witnesses,—a due sense of obedience to whatever obligations he has voluntarily assumed towards the United States with reference to Spain, under his petition and oath of naturalization, until the contrary is made to appear. In this instance, there is no evidence or suggestion growing out of the facts of the case that Mr. Sanguily has manifested toward the Spanish authorities in Cuba any hostility, ill feeling, or want of due respect to the laws. In all respects he has been true to his duty to the United States, while residing in Cuba, his native country, under the passport and registry of the United States and also of Cuba,

---

(*) The report was submitted on February 24, 1897. It was then ordered to be printed; and it was printed and distributed in the Senate Chamber on February 25th, when it was taken up. The Honorable Mr. George F. Hoar, from Massachusetts, got up and said: "I desire to know whether the report which has been within sixty seconds, or thereabout, laid on my desk, is the report upon this case?" He being assured that it was, added :—"It has just come from the printer. It is a report of 96 pages. I desire to ask the Senator (the Honorable Mr. Morgan) if he does not think the members of the Senate ought to have an opportunity to read the report before they act upon the joint resolution, and that the matter ought to go over long enough to enable us to read it?—I never have seen it before." (Congressional Record, February 25, 1897, page 2379.)

and the only ground of proceeding against him in Cuba has been an unjust suspicion, derived from the honorable and devotional courage he exhibited in his efforts to free Cuba from Spanish dominion in the former revolution that ended nearly twenty years ago."

At the conclusion of this extraordinary debate, the joint resolution was reported to the Senate without amendments (Congressional Record, February 25, 1897, page 2392), and then and there the matter ended. The Honorable Mr. Stephen M. White, of California, addressed the Senate for some time, and the debate went over to the following day, when the Honorable Mr. George Gray, from Delaware, formally informed the Senate that Julio Sanguily had been released, and that no further action in regard to this matter was therefore necessary. "Sanguily has been released," said the Honorable Senator, "and thanks to God is to-day a free man. So much has been accomplished by an American Secretary of State, who throughout all this business has never failed to assert the rights and dignity of this country in behalf of this Spanish-American citizen."

During the course of the discussion on the 25th of February, 1897, the writer of these pages, feeling apprehensive as to the effect which the action of the Senate in Committee of the Whole might produce both in Cuba and in Madrid, deemed it to be his duty to address himself to the Honorable Chairman of the Committee on Foreign Relations of that distinguished body, and request in his client's name the suspension of a movement which endangered his liberty. He went to the Senate Chamber, and having been granted there the honor and the favor of a personal interview with that distinguished Senator, explained to him verbally what the real situation of the case was in Havana, and how perhaps at that very moment, as it proved exactly to be the fact, the order for the release of the prisoner had already reached there. In addition to these statements, which the distinguished Senator kindly listened

to and considered, the writer of these pages left in his hands
the following letter :

WASHINGTON, D. C.,
February 25th, 1897.

HONORABLE JOHN SHERMAN,
Chairman of the Senate Committee
of Foreign Relations, etc., etc., etc.

Sir :—Shall I be permitted, in my capacity of counsel and
representative of Mr. Julio Sanguily, imprisoned in Havana,
to request you, in all earnest, in the name of my client, and for
his benefit, to prevent, if possible, the passage of the resolution
directing a demand to be made upon the Spanish Government
for the release of my client ?

Said release having been already granted by the Spanish
Government, upon no other condition than the fulfilment of a
certain technical requirement of the Spanish law, a condition
to which I here, and Sanguily's lawyer in Havana, do readily
assent : would it not be injurious to the prisoner to afford the
Spanish Government a plausible opportunity to withdraw from
its engagement in this respect ?

Of course, I can not but be grateful to the generous spirit
shown by the resolution to which I refer,—as I am with all
my heart, and my client is, grateful to the Honorable Secretary
of State for his manly, untiring and benevolent efforts in favor
of Mr. Sanguily.  I can not but see and recognize that the
movement in the Senate is inspired in the same generous feeling
which from the beginning has inspired the Honorable Secretary
of State.  But I am afraid that the effect which the resolution,
if passed, will necessarily produce in the Government circles of
Spain, and perhaps among the masses, will result in the defeat
of the efforts, both of the State Department and of the Senate.

I make to you therefore an earnest appeal, in the name of
Mr. Sanguily, to submit this letter, if proper, to the consideration of the Senate, which in its wisdom will no doubt pay
attention to the statements therein contained

I am, sir, with the greatest respect
Your obedient servant,
J. I. RODRIGUEZ,
*Counsel for Julio Sanguily.*


The announcement made by the Honorable Senator from
Delaware, Mr. George Gray, caused, as it was natural, the
whole matter to stop.  There was, of course, some show of

the disappointment felt by some political opponents of the Honorable Secretary of State, in seeing, that his wise and patriotic action had been vindicated by that greatest of human tests which is called success, and that therefore the possibility to harrass him in this respect had vanished. But beyond some weak expressions of that feeling, nothing else was done, except the presentation by the Honorable Mr. John W. Daniel, from Virginia, of a document which contradicts the so-called statement of facts presented to the Senate by the Honorable Mr. Call, on January 7th, 1897, in the part thereof which refers to the place of naturalization of Sanguily. This document is a certified copy of the record of Sanguily's naturalization, on August 6th, 1878, in the Superior Court of the City of New York, under Section 2167 of the Revised Statutes of the United States, commonly known by the name of the "Law of minors."

The Honorable Senator requested that this certified copy should be printed in the Record, and so it was ordered and done. (Congressional Record, February 27th, 1897, page 2404.)

## XII.

### COMPARISON BETWEEN THE CASE OF JULIO SANGUILY AND OTHER CASES OF SIMILAR CHARACTER.

*I. The Trasher Case.*

MR. JOHN SIDNEY TRASHER, a native of the city of Portland, in the State of Maine, of the United States of America, residing in Havana, was arrested on the 16th of October, 1851, tried for alleged "treason" to the Spanish Government by a military tribunal, namely the Permanent and Executive Military Commission of the Island of Cuba, and condemned, on the 16th of November following, to imprisonment for eight years in chains and at hard labor in the penal settlement of Ceuta, in northern Africa.

The State Department, at whose head was at that time a man of such force and pronounced Americanism as the great Daniel Webster, did not accede however to interfere in behalf of the prisoner, or to urge that the privileges of Article VII of the treaty of 1795, should be extended to him. The action which he took, and indeed most reluctantly, was in favor of a pardon, and gave up from the outset the great point upon which the intervention by the Government of the United States could only be warranted. Mr. Webster explained in his remarkable report of December 23rd, 1851 (Executive Document No. 10, House of Representatives, 32nd Congress, 1st Session pages from 2 to 7), that while there was " no doubt that John S. Trasher is a citizen of the United States by birth," even admitting that the treaty between the United States and Spain granted such privileges as were claimed by the prisoner and his friends, the point still remained to be settled whether those rights secured by treaty, "be not justly limited to such persons as are, at the time, in all respects, American citizens, having never voluntarily changed their domicile, or taken upon themselves a new allegiance."

In fact it might be said, that Mr. Webster would not have interfered at all in this business, if Mr. Daniel M. Barringer, United States Minister at Madrid, would have not ventured to take up the subject there "without official instructions" (Mr. Barringer to Mr. Webster, January 14, 1852, Executive Document, No. 86, House of Representatives, 33d Congress, 1st session, page 106), and succeeded in persuading the Spanish Government to apply to Mr. Trasher the benefits of a general amnesty granted in those days by Her Majesty the Queen of Spain.

The Cuban question at that time was not less prominently than now before the eyes of the American statesmen, and the friends of Mr. Trasher had taken all the advantage that the circumstances afforded them to create agitation. The public press had not been negligent in helping Mr. Trasher's cause, and his friends in Congress had also done their best. A resolution was passed, on the 15th of December, 1851, by the House of Representatives of the United States, "requesting the President, so far as in his judgment may be compatible with the public interest, to communicate to the House any information in possession of the Executive respecting the imprisonment, trial and sentence of John S. Trasher in the Island of Cuba, and to his right to claim the protection of the Government as a native born citizen of the United States;" and the President in response to this resolution sent first a report from Mr. Webster, Secretary of State (the report to which reference has been made before) and the papers which together with it were printed and are known as "Executive Document, No. 10, House of Representatives, 32nd Congress, 1st session, Information respecting the imprisonment, etc., of John S. Trasher." Additional papers were transmitted on January 2nd, 1852, which were likewise printed and form "Executive Document No. 14, House of Representatives, 32nd Congress, 1st session, Further information respecting the imprisonment, etc., of John S. Trasher."

In April, 1854, still further information was forwarded to the House of Representatives, as enclosures to a report from the Secretary of State, Mr. W. L. Marcy, to the President of the United States "in regard to Spanish violations of the rights of American citizens."—Executive Document No. 86, House of Representatives, 33rd Congress, 1st session.—The papers relating to Mr. Trasher's case included in this volume can be found from page 105 to page 127.

Mr. Trasher himself, who always was loud in his denunciation of the treatment to which he was submitted, had caused his Appeal to the Government of the United States and to his fellow-citizens, written "in a dungeon of the Punta Castle," Havana, November 21st, 1851 (Ex. Doc. No. 14, House of Representatives, 32nd Congress, 1st session, pages 6 to 8), to be published and widely circulated in the United States.

And Mr. Allen F. Owen, who was then the United States Consul at Havana, had been so diligent and energetic in defending the rights of Mr. Trasher, that the Governor-General of Cuba told him officially, November 23rd, 1851. "You are well aware that Consuls are nothing else than mere commercial agents, and I nothing more than a deputy of the Spanish Government in this province. The complaints and reclamations of Mr. J. S. Trasher are therefore out of the sphere of those reclamations which you, in the exercise of your consular functions, have the power to prefer. My duty could never permit me to answer to them." (Executive Document No. 10, House of Representatives, 32nd Congress, 1st session, page 20.) Marquis Miraflores, the Spanish Secretary of State, in writing to Mr. Barringer, the United States Minister at Madrid, August 20th, 1851, explained to him that the Captain-General of Cuba had the power "to suspend" a Consul, and "even to compel him to leave the Island, without such an act being considered as an infringement of the respect due to the Government which he serves," and suggested in consequence "the propriety of Mr. Allen F. Owen's making himself thoroughly acquainted with the nature and extent of his duties." (*Ibid*, page 10.)

In spite of all this, Mr. Webster, while yielding as he said to the pressure of Mr. Trasher's friends, not without explaining the reason why he believed that Mr. Trasher ought not to be protected (Mr. Webster to Mr. Barringer, December 13th, 1851, *Ibid*, pages 30–32),—confined his action, as above stated, to instruct Mr. Barringer to recommend to the Spanish Government "the expediency of pardoning" Mr. Trasher.

When these instructions reached Madrid, Mr. Barringer had done *motu proprio*, and done successfully, what in this note he was told to do.

And now comes another feature which strongly contrasts this case with the case of Sanguily. Not only was the latter much better protected by the State Department than Mr. Trasher was, but special care was taken from saving him from humiliations and sufferings which Mr. Trasher could not escape.

Mr. Trasher was not pardoned until after he had been made to travel, in irons, as a convict, from Havana to Vigo, from Vigo to Cadiz, and from Cadiz to Ceuta, and until he had entered the African penal establishment, and had had his hair cropped, his face clean shaved, his body dressed in the convict's attire, his limbs burdened with the regulation fetters, and his soul afflicted by tremendous humiliation and agony.

Fourteen months after his release, when the administration had been changed, and Mr. W. L. Marcy was Secretary of State, Mr. Trasher presented a claim against the Spanish Government asking for an indemnity to the amount of $350,000.00. His letter was endorsed by Mr. John L. Hayes, and Mr. Alexander N. Lawrence, counsellors at law in the City of Washington, as the claimant's attorneys. (Executive Document No. 86, House of Representatives, 33d Congress, 1st session, page 125 and the following.)

It appears that this claim was admitted in principle, as there is a letter in which Mr. Marcy informed one of the lawyers of Mr. Trasher that a proposition had " been recently made to Spain and other powers for the organization of a board for the mutual adjustment of all existing claims between the respective Governments." (*Ibid*, page 127.)

Seven years, afterwards, March 5th, 1860, a convention was concluded in Madrid between the Governments of the United States and Spain, establishing a joint Commission for the final adjudication and payment of all the claims of the respective parties,—a convention by which, according to Dr. Wharton's authorized opinion, "the validity and amount of the Cuban claims were expressly admitted and their speedy payment was placed beyond question." The negotiation failed, however, because the Senate of the United States "greatly to the surprise of the President and the disappointment of the claimants" refused to approve the convention.—(Dr. Wharton's, Digest of the International Law of the United States, section 38, Vol. I, page 164.)

Whether Mr. Trasher's claim was included in that arrangement, or whether it is still in abeyance and waiting with the others, which the failure of the convention left again *in nubibus*, or whether it was acted upon in some other way, the writer of these pages does not know.

The fact has been mentioned only to demonstrate that the opinion so absolutely and dogmatically maintained by the Honorable Mr. Wm. P. Fry, in the Senate of the United States, on the 25th of February, 1897, that the granting of a pardon involves for the pardoned man and his family the loss of all claims whatever for damages, was not shared on this occasion either by his fellow-citizen from Maine, Mr. Trasher, his attorneys, Mr. Alexander N. Lawrence, and Mr. John L. Hayes, or perhaps Mr. Marcy himself. Even if it were true, absolutely, that a pardon has the effect attributed to it by the distinguished Senator from Maine, the slightest investigation of the subject might have shown him that one thing is a pardon, by which the penalties of a sentence are wiped out, and another thing is a commutation of a sentence, by which a penalty is imposed in place of another.

*II. The Houard Case.*

MR. JOHN EMILIO HOUARD, a native of the City of Philadelphia, in the State of Pennsylvania, of the United States
of America, residing in Cienfuegos, Island of Cuba, where he
was engaged in the practice of medicine, was arrested on the
20th of July, 1871, tried by a council of war, on the charge of
being in sympathy with the insurgents, and having given
them money and medicines (*), and sentenced on December
15th, 1871, to imprisonment for eight years in chains and at
hard labor in the penal settlement of Ceuta in northern Africa,
and to the confiscation of his property.

The State Department, at whose head was at that time a man
so prominent and conspicuous in the History of the United
States as the Honorable Mr. Hamilton Fish, of New York,
was, did not feel much more affected by Dr. Houard's mis-
fortunes, than it formerly had been by Mr. Trasher's.

Friends and relations of Dr. Houard urged the Honorable
Mr. Hamilton Fish to protect the prisoner. A number of
trustworthy citizens of Philadelphia sent to him a memorial
requesting him to take action for the discharge of Dr. Houard
from his confinement. The Vice President of the United
States, Mr. Schuyler Colfax, put himself personally in communication with him respecting this business. And the House
of Representatives of the United States passed a resolution
(March 19th, 1872) requesting the President to communicate
to that body, "if not incompatible with the public interest all
the information in possession of the Government relative to the
case of Dr. J. E. Houard, a native of Philadelphia, and a citizen
of the United States, now held by the Spanish authorities on
the Island of Cuba, and what steps, if any, have been taken to
protect the rights of this American citizen, who it is alleged
from various respectable sources has been unjustly arrested,

---

(*) The latter charge rested on the fact that a small box of homeopathic
medicines, on the interior of which the Doctor's name was stamped, was
found by a Spanish column, in a rebel encampment.

condemned and transported to a penal settlement on the coast
of Africa."

In addition to this resolution, the Honorable Mr. Samuel J.
Randall, of Pennsylvania, introduced on April 8, 1872, another
one which recited at length the wrongs done to Dr. Houard,
and ended by declaring that in the judgment of the House the
President should promptly demand his unconditional release
and the return of his confiscated property.

In response to the resolution of the House, the President sent
the papers which were printed and form: (1) Executive Document No. 223, House of Representatives, 42nd Congress, 2nd
session; (2) Executive Document No. 223, part 2nd, House of
Representatives, 42nd Congress, 2nd session; and (3) Miscel-
laneous Document No. 188, House of Representatives, 42nd
Congress, 2nd session.

Mr. Alfred T. A. Torbert, who was then the United States
Consul-General at Havana, and who as shown by his despatch
of February 19, 1872 (Executive Document No. 223, House
of Representatives, 42nd Congress, 2nd session, page 125),
entertained an opinion as to Dr. Houard's American citizenship, different from that of the Honorable Mr. Hamilton Fish,
interposed all his influence with the Governor-General of Cuba,
in favor of Dr. Houard, who to his judgment was "beyond
a doubt" a citizen of the United States of America, and succeeded in securing that the prisoner, who had already "his
beard and hair cut off" and donned "the prison garb,"
"would not be sent to work outside of the prison."

In his letter to Vice President Colfax the Honorable Mr.
Hamilton Fish alleged against the claim of American citizenship made by Dr. Houard and his friends, that it did not
appear that Dr. Houard "interested himself, as did so many
citizens at home and abroad, in behalf of the union cause during our own war, that he offered his services as surgeon in our
volunteer army, that he subscribed to any of the war charities,
or that he paid at any time income tax or other tax to the

United States." (Executive Document No. 223, House of Representatives, 42nd Congress, 2nd session, page 29.) And what was still worse for the prisoner, the Honorable Mr. Hamilton Fish went further on and said : " The strong point which prevents the intervention of this Government in behalf of Dr. Houard from being efficacious for his release is the fact that he has been regularly tried and found guilty by a duly constituted tribunal in the Island of Cuba." (*Ibid*, page 29.)(*)

It will be seen without difficulty that while opinions of this kind prevailed at the State Department, the action of the latter in favor of the prisoner was necessarily lukewarm. There was nevertheless at that time at Madrid, as diplomatic representative of the United States, such a strong and able man as General Daniel E. Sickles, and through his efforts, not entirely unaided by the unexpected appearance of an American man-of-war at the port of Cadiz, a pardon was granted to Dr. Houard, who was already at Ceuta. Don Cristino Martos, Spanish Secretary of State, informed General Sickles of the decision reached, on July 4th, 1872; but it took a long while for the orders to reach the penal settlement, and Dr. Houard was not actually released until the 1st of August, 1872.

One year afterwards, Doctor Houard presented a claim for damages against the Government of Spain, and asked for an indemnity of $50,000. The Honorable Mr. Hamilton Fish referred this claim to the United States and Spanish Claims Commission of Arbitration, which some time before had been established in Washington, and there it was entered under No. 107. The Advocate of the United States, who was then the learned and distinguished jurist, Mr. Thomas J. Durant, defended the case and attended to the rights of the claimant and of the United States in his behalf, as zealously and ably as he always did. The American Arbitrator recognized the validity of the claim and made an award for $50,000. The

(*) The record of this trial before a Council of War is on the files of the United States and American Claims Commission of 1871-83, case No. 107.

Arbitrator for Spain disagreed and dismissed the case. The Umpire who was then Baron Blanc, the Italian Minister in Washington, was called therefore to decide the case ; but that distinguished gentleman, as set forth in his opinion of February 4th, 1880,—fully eight years after the presentation of the case,—launched the claim out of existence on the following grounds :

"The Umpire does not deem it consistent with the character of his office, nor required by the interests of either party, that the questions involved in the sentence, those disposed of heretofore and intended to be closed by a conditional pardon granted as the result of an international agreement should now be reopened. With this view of the case it is unnecessary to determine whether or not (*) the alleged loss of claimant's nationality of origin by expatriation is sustained. On the other ground above stated the Umpire must hold against the claimant and therefore dismisses the claim."

The Umpire said, however, that "the injustice complained of (by the claimant) is hardly open to dispute."

## III. The Pouble Case.

MR. CIRILO POUBLE, a naturalized citizen of the United States, residing in New York, went to Cuba, with an American passport, vised by the Spanish Consul at Key West, Fla., and was arrested at the very moment of his arrival at Havana on the 23d of November, 1884. The Spanish Consul after viséing his passport informed the Cuban authorities that Mr. Pouble was going there, and they waited for him, and put him under arrest as soon as he landed.

They searched his baggage, and found nothing either in his trunk or about his person.

---

(*) The determination of this question was however the only duty devolved upon the Umpire under the agreement which created the Commission.

From there he was taken to the public jail and then to a cell in the *La Punta* Castle situated at the entrance of the Havana harbor.

His offense consisted in having been the editor, in the City of New York, of a newspaper, printed in the Spanish language, and called *El Separatista,*—a paper which was no longer in existence, and which had strenuously advocated the cessation of the Spanish rule in Cuba,—in having been a member of a political club established in New York devoted to the propagation of the same ideas,—and in having issued, or signed, while in the United States, as member of that club, or in some other capacity, certain printed blanks of commissions to serve in the revolutionary Cuban army.

The Spanish authorities of Cuba did not make any effort to contradict Mr. Pouble's American citizenship, and decided to try him by civil jurisdiction under the terms of the Cushing-Calderón y Collantes Protocol, and according to the provisions of the Law of April 17th, 1821. At the end of thirty-two months (August 10th, 1886), a sentence was passed by the Court, which condemned Mr. Pouble to imprisonment for life at hard labor.

This most remarkable case attracted in its day to considerable extent the attention of the public. The claim that Mr. Pouble was liable to punishment by the Spanish authorities in Cuba, when caught there, for alleged offenses against her, committed, if committed at all, outside of the Spanish territory, involved an assertion of extra-territorial jurisdiction which could not be easily acquiesced by the people of this country. The arguments that the result of the offense committed here was to have its effect there,—and that promoting here ill feeling against Spain was equivalent to making war against her, which a private citizen certainly cannot do,—were strained to such an undue extent, that all their force was lost.

The friends of Mr. Pouble, and the writer of these pages, as Mr. Pouble's counsel, exhausted all the means which were at their disposal for the relief of the prisoner. Nothing could be obtained from the State Department; but the Senate of the United States, whose attention was called to the subject by means of a memorial, took not entirely without effect, some notice of the case. The Senate Committee on Foreign Relations reported, on March 24, 1886, that there is nothing that at present calls for any action on the part of the Senate, or of Congress. But, "if there should be much further delay in the trial of Pouble, it will become a subject for very serious consideration on the part of the Government of the United States." (Senate Report No. 275, 49th Congress, 1st session.)

An effort was then made to release Mr. Pouble by imploring his pardon, but not even this movement was undertaken by the Honorable Mr. Frederick T. Frelinghuysen or fostered with his assistance.

A sister of the prisoner was requested by the friends of the latter, to file a petition to the Supreme Government of Spain, requesting the pardon of her brother; and the United States Consul-General at Havana, Mr. R. O. Williams, interposed in great earnest all his personal influence with the Governor-General to secure, as he did, that the petition should be sent to Madrid, with favorable recommendation. On October 25th, 1888, he was still working, together with the writer of these pages, in securing the desired release (*). But the pardon was not granted until the 23rd of January, 1889; and then Mr. Pouble, after four years and two months of imprisonment in La Punta Castle was set at liberty.

---

(*) Mr. Williams addressed then to the writer of these pages the following letter:

HAVANA, October 25, 1888.

MY DEAR MR. RODRIGUEZ:

I am glad to be able to inform you that the petition of Miss Pouble has been most favorably reported upon by the authorities having cognizance of the matter, and that it goes forward to Spain to-day endorsed by the hearty recommendation of the Governor-General in favor of the pardon of her brother Mr. Cirilo Pouble.

I am, yours very truly,

J. I. RODRIGUEZ, ESQ.,  RAMON O. WILLIAMS.
Ebbitt House,
Washington, D. C.

## CONCLUSION.

The reader of these pages will find out, without difficulty, especially if he is in any way conversant with public affairs, or if he feels some interest, whether professional, political, or merely historical, in the subject to which they refer, that the lessons to be taught by the study of the Sanguily case are in numerous respects exceedingly important. And indeed, were it not for this reason, the excuse for increasing, with this new allusion to a case finally disposed of, the burden already ponderous of the juridical and diplomatic literature of the day, would be rather flimsy.

One aspect more than others commends the case especially to the attention of students,—and it is the close resemblance which it bears, from its inception to its end, and through all its different evolutions, to the general perplexing and most involved political and social problem of the Island of Cuba,—a resemblance which increases the interest to be felt in its study, as it takes away from the subject its individual character and raises it up to higher grounds, where universal justice and far sighted statesmanship can be called into exercise.

The Sanguily case reveals, prominently above all its other features, and in the most striking similitude with all the phases of the political situation in Cuba, ever since 1825, that a feeling of deeply rooted, almost invincible distrust, capable to put down and smother all sentiment of kinship, good will or even magnanimity,— is the prevailing element in the relations between Spain and Cuba. It shows, also in common with the Cuban question, that this nefarious, sterilizing sentiment, causes wrongs to be done, even in spite of generous impulses, and prevents them from being righted, except, if ever, at a late hour, through outside pressure, and in a manner calculated to produce no lasting effect. It bears testimony, exactly the same as the Cuban problem, to the fact, whether willingly or unwillingly accepted, and each time better established, that in all questions concerning the action of Spain in this continent the United States of America are a party to the contention,—and that in obedience to eternal laws, historical and social, as inevitable in their effect as the laws of Nature, the wishes of the Government of the United States of America have always to prevail in the end.  And it shows, in fine, and in no lesser a degree than the Cuban problem, that all attempt, no matter how much accompanied by noise and alleged popular support, to force upon the administration, an undesired attitude, or to dictate to it the manner and the form in which its duty must be performed,—is foolish to the extreme, and dangerous even if it is sincere.

There is an incident in the military career of Julio Sanguily, to which his brother Don Manuel, with all the fervor of his eloquence made a brilliant allusion at the banquet given by some friends of the former in the city of Philadelphia, Pa., in celebration of his freedom and his return to the United States. The distinguished orator compared what he called "the first rescue" of his brother,—when the latter prostrated by the enemy at an encounter during the ten years war, and made a prisoner and wounded, and tied to the back of a horse, and carried in this way to some safe place of imprisonment, or perhaps to the scaffold, was restored to liberty by the sudden appearance of the heroical Cuban General Don Ignacio Agramonte, who with characteristic impetuosity threw himself in the midst of the group of soldiers who surrounded his helpless friend and attacked them and caused them to fly in terror and abandon their prey,—with what he called very properly "the second rescue," when the American eagle snatched him again out of the hands of his enemies and opened for him the gates of the prison.

The writer of these pages was not present at that festivity, but what he learned of this well devised comparison impressed him by its correctness.   Had it not been for this giant, who is called the American Government: had it happened for its executive and diplomatic department to be entrusted to less faithful hands, or to persons of less supreme manliness and political honesty than President Cleveland and his Secretary of State, Mr. Olney, the fate of Sanguily would have been very different. Thanks to the courage of those two great Americans, to their wonderful power of resistance to improper pressure from whatever side, and to their kindness towards the prisoner in whom they saw only a fellow-citizen, Julio Sanguily is not still lingering inside a Spanish fortress, or serving a sentence as cruel as ignominious.

It was printed by the Washington *Post*, in its edition of the 4th of March, 1897, in a review of " Mr. Cleveland's second term as President," that "if there were nothing else to the credit of his administration, the diplomatic victory obtained by Secretary Olney over the British Foreign Office in a series of masterly dispatches (the Venezuelan affair), would suffice to set off'' all errors or shortcomings, if any, which might be found. "But this glorious chapter," the paper further said "is happily not alone. By its side must be placed the negotiation of the general arbitration treaty, which no matter when, or in what manner ratified," (or rejected the writer of these pages says) "must always stand as another monument to the skill and power of Secretary Olney."

The release of Sanguily stands also by its side; and so stand other victories, and more than all the cessation of the system and of the influences which for long time before had made Spain almost omnipotent in Washington.

The intervention of the Achilles of the Cuban war of 1868-1878 saved Sanguily upon the field of battle. The intervention of the Achilles of the American diplomacy saved him now from his enemies and perhaps also from his friends.